Challenging Homophobia:
teaching about Sexual Diversity

*edited by Lutz van Dijk and
Barry van Driel*

Foreword by Desmond Tutu

Trentham Books

Stoke on Trent, UK and Sterling, USA

Trentham Books Limited
Westview House   22883 Quicksilver Drive
734 London Road   Sterling
Oakhill   VA 20166-2012
Stoke on Trent   USA
Staffordshire
England ST4 5NP

Cover: Fiona Passantino

First published 2007

British Library Cataloguing-in-Publication Data
A catalogue record for this book is available from the
British Library

ISBN: 978 1 85856 413 5

Designed and typeset by Trentham Print Design Ltd,
Chester and printed in Great Britain by Cromwell
Press Ltd, Trowbridge.

Contents

Foreword
Homophobia is a crime against humanity
Archbishop emeritus Desmond Mpilo Tutu

The voices of homophobia are still strong in this world: from Burma to Indonesia, from Mexico to Peru, from the USA to Russia, from Egypt to Iran, from the UK to Poland, from India to Nigeria the voices of fear, hate and persecution are often supported by political and faith leaders.

The discrimination and persecution of people because of their sexual orientation is as unjust as the crime of racism. Homophobia is a crime against humanity. We overcame apartheid. We will overcome homophobia.

It is indeed a matter of ordinary justice. We struggled against apartheid in South Africa, supported by people the world over, because black people were being blamed for something we could do nothing about – our very skins. It is the same with sexual orientation. It is a given. I could not have fought against the discrimination of apartheid and not also fight against the discrimination of homophobia.

Hatred and prejudice are such destructive forces. They destroy human beings, communities and whole societies. And they destroy the hater too, from the inside. A parent who brings up a child to be racist damages that child and damages the community in which they live. A teacher who educates a child to believe that there is only one sexual orientation and that anything else is evil denies our humanity and their own too.

This book is edited by Lutz van Dijk from South Africa and Barry van Driel from the Netherlands, both known as longstanding human rights activists, one with a gay, one with a straight sexual orientation. They present not only a most inspiring collection of international experiences on how to overcome homophobia in educational practice but also demonstrate by their collaboration how schools and universities can become kind and respectful learning environments.

It will never work to answer hate with hate. To educate children to embrace diversity will enable all of them to enjoy life and to contribute towards a world with more justice, peace and humanity.

Archbishop Emeritus Desmond Mpilo Tutu, born 1931 in South Africa, Nobel Peace Prize Laureate in 1984, was chairman of the South African Truth and Reconciliation Commission 1996-1998.

Introduction
Being straight – being gay:
the perspectives of the Editors

Lutz van Dijk and Barry van Driel

Certainly, the two of us have a lot in common: We are the same generation, we started working at the Anne Frank House in Amsterdam in the same year, collaborating on teacher training around intercultural education for several years. Both of us lived for part of our lives in different countries, even different continents and our families have mixed cultural and national backgrounds. We are both white males and academics who had the privilege of a good education in the richer parts of our planet. Finally, we both enjoy happy relationships, children included – and here it might end: Barry is married to his wife and lives in Belgium, Lutz has a registered partnership with his man in South Africa.

There is much to say about the editors' professional challenge in putting this book together: we can't fall back on a sound academic discussion, not even on much international research into tackling homophobia in schools. We are aware that the entire concept of homophobia is a limited one which might not be seen as relevant, let alone understood or accepted, in many parts of the world. Wouldn't it have been better to call the book *Dealing with sexual diversity in schools* or *How to support sexual minorities in the classroom?* Maybe.

The various approaches have their distinct advantages and disadvantages. We are grateful to all our authors for accepting our offer to join us on a road which hasn't been travelled much, which still has its shortcomings and surprises. What all the authors in this book share is a commitment to combat a phenomenon that causes pain for millions of innocent young men and woman around the world: young people who are discriminated against or even violently attacked because of widespread homophobia in society and in our schools.

Before we explain the choice of contributions and the content of each chapter, it might contribute to the honesty of this book to tell something about the personal background of the editors and why we decided to work on this book together.

Barry van Driel

Why on earth would the hetero white guy want to write a book on homophobia? Is it some kind of hetero guilt, some latent homosexual feelings or some desire to be politically correct? I am going to make the assumption that none of the above are true.

Instead, I have to delve into both my personal past and my professional work.

My life has been relatively easy when it comes to sexual identity and sexual behaviour. Being straight and acting straight is so automatic and so accepted that I rarely think about my sexual identity – or my white identity for that matter. But, as a young man, I had the good fortune to be invited to gay parties and get-togethers by trusted friends. I have to admit that initially I felt out of place and uncomfortable. Though I thought I had no problems with gays and lesbians, I was troubled by my discomfort. As a straight white guy I am not accustomed to being approached in an assertive sexual way, either by men or by women. All I took for granted about the world around me, the heterosexual world, was suddenly questioned – something which had never happened before in school, in my family, in the media or anywhere else. As straights, I think most of us would benefit from experiences that challenge our assumptions in profound ways. Only then can we realise how things we have taken for granted our entire life are anything but automatic and can actually oppress others in subtle and sometimes not so subtle ways.

I have a cousin and another member of the family who are gay but have not come out. One family is progressive, politically at least, and living in the Netherlands and the other family is staunchly Catholic and lives in the Southern USA. But both respond to their son's homosexuality in a similar way

– by ignoring it and on occasion denying it. My aunt and uncle (the progressives) for years simply said that my cousin had just not met the right woman yet. Well, he is now almost 40... In fact on every family occasion I attended over the years, both men refused to talk about the subject. They obviously had their reasons. And still have.

Why do I think differently from my relatives? I am not sure. Perhaps it is because my parents were immigrants and taught me that I should ignore the comments we sometimes heard about our background and that I should not be ashamed of who I was. We were not to blame for the negative comments we had thrown at us from time to time. I think this made me sensitive to all those who have to struggle to be accepted simply because of who they are.

My work life has added a further reason to write about homophobia. A few years ago I was coordinating a large educational project that brought together human rights educators from around Europe. I made the assumption that I was therefore dealing with people who shared a common understanding when it came to issues of tolerance, intolerance and respect. One day I proudly took them to the Homomonument in Amsterdam, right next to the Anne Frank House, which commemorates all 'homosexual women and men who have suffered persecution in the past, who continue to suffer persecution in the present and who will suffer in the future'.

I remember there being only silence as I explained the significance of the monument. Then the Romanian educator turned to me and said: 'That is disgusting'. I thought she meant the persecution of gays, but she clearly meant the monument. The educator from Armenia chimed in: 'That is against nature and God'. I started to engage with them but quickly discovered that it was hard to argue rationally against educators who held totally irrational views on the topic, quoting the Bible as their ultimate source of understanding. Who was I to argue against the word of God? I still get upset if I think about the many young people, of whichever sexual orientation, who might turn to these two educators for guidance on issues of human rights.

Recently I was in Minneapolis, Minnesota, to give a workshop on the Holocaust and human rights. The main resource was a manual on different aspects of this history. The manual contained various references to the Nazi persecution of gays. The organisers were happy that the manual also focused on other victims of Nazi persecution. But one of the sponsors, a local school district, sent a letter asking for clarification as to why 'homosexuals were mentioned'. They made it clear that they did not want to see their teachers 'exposed' to this information. They asked us to downplay this part of the manual and stated that they would glue the relevant pages together for their district so their teachers would not be 'exposed'. We made it clear that we would *not* downplay the information and would work with the full manual, perhaps paying even greater attention to those parts because of the homophobia in contemporary society. The school district subsequently withdrew its support. On a positive note, about eight teachers went against the decision of the school district, took vacation time and attended anyway.

Throughout my professional life, mainly working around issues of the Holocaust and human rights, I have encountered resistance from people I assumed were allies in the struggle to promote human rights for all. I have been left with the nagging feeling that I need more tools to address the pervasive homophobia around me, in my extended family and in my professional contacts. For me this book is an attempt to bring together some international experts to reflect on how we can better arm ourselves to combat homophobia in different contexts. How do I effectively confront those who turn to an ultimate source like the Bible or Q'uran? How do I give effective support to teachers and students who want to combat the homophobia at their schools – or their own heterosexual biases?

I had only known Lutz van Dijk for a short while when, many years ago, he gave a workshop for a large group of German teachers on the persecution of lesbians and gays, past and present. He introduced historical documents I had not even been aware of although I had been busy with the history of World War II for many years. At one stage he simply asked the participants how their families and friends would respond if they came home and said that they were gay or lesbian. One could almost hear the brain cells and neurons clicking into action. As they sat there, their facial muscles betrayed a range of emotions: disgust, humour, fear, anger and shock could all be felt in the room. Most verbal responses that followed were rational and articulate – the teachers had regained their composure and did well at covering up any emotions. But the earlier body language had betrayed that something significant had happened. I realised at that moment that the topic is emotionally loaded and that with the right tools one could touch and stir those emotions, which would perhaps be a good first step in changing attitudes.

When I got the idea of compiling a book on the topic of challenging homophobia I had no doubt about my first choice as a co-editor.

Lutz van Dijk

The first difference between Barry's and my life while growing up: for me, nothing could be taken for granted. I knew I was different long before I had a word for it, long before I could attach it to sexuality at all.

Like everybody else, sexuality is just one part of my personality, an important part, but not everything. I always struggled not to be reduced to just a 'gay activist' although there have been periods in my life when I have felt forced to speak out – as a matter of self-respect and survival.

When I was a child homosexuality between men was still a crime in Germany, so there was much silence around the topic. One distant uncle committed suicide and the rumour went round that he was 'so'. As a student I had an affair with another young man and one day we were attacked by a group of drunken straight guys. Not in any dark place or so-called cruising area but on a crowded promenade on a warm summer evening. Everybody looked on, no one helped. For the first time I decided to fight back. I got off lightly, but my friend had to be admitted to hospital. I joined one of the first local gay rights groups as one of its youngest members.

This pattern repeated itself many times in my life: I always focused on developing as a whole human being. I travelled a lot and tried my best to learn languages. I studied education and history. But when I was challenged I acted.

Decades passed: When I was awarded a Youth Literature Award in Namibia, Southern Africa, in 1997, I was also invited to be the keynote speaker on human rights as the honoured book dealt with racism. The then president of Namibia, Sam Nujoma, had just declared that homosexuality 'is the devil at work' – as his neighbour and 'comrade' Zimbabwean president Robert Mugabe had said about lesbians and gays 'that they are worse than dogs and pigs' because the animals at least know how to behave in their own group. I decided to criticise his statements, but politely. He wasn't present himself, but some ministers and many ambassadors were. It resulted in a vibrant tumult and some threats. The chair of the event refused to hand over the medal as she obviously assumed that all male homosexuals are infected with HIV and – as she put it – she didn't 'want to be infected by a gay with AIDS'. However, several Namibian youth groups expressed their gratitude for my talk.

There is one exception to my being forced to take action – my writing. This is my joy and free choice. It was choice to write my book for young readers *Damned Strong Love* (van Dijk, 1995 and 2003 a/b). This is based on a true story and translated into several languages. It is about the Polish teenager Stefan who falls in love with a young German soldier in occupied Poland during World War II. What a privilege to discover Stefan T. Kosinski and to work on the book together with the old gentleman in Warsaw and listen to his stories of surviving Nazi concentration camps. The many readings I gave from the book in schools in several countries were truly an enrichment of my life. To my knowledge it is still the only book for young readers on the subject in the world. The special friendship with Stefan until his death in 2003 has contributed to my own identity as a gay man.

It led indirectly to my involvement in organising, in cooperation with Amnesty International and the Dutch Foreign Ministry, the Human Rights Storytelling Festival during the Gay Games 1998 in Amsterdam with young women and men from more than 30 countries, some of which still have the death penalty for homosexuality today. Over three evenings mostly young women and men from Latin America, Asia, Africa, several Islamic countries and Eastern Europe gave their personal accounts to a deeply moved audience in a packed hall. Some came out in public for the first time ever, some received standing ovations for minutes. With the assistance of several Dutch embassies we did our best to assure the personal safety of all the participants. Some had to travel via third countries so as not to endanger their lives.

One woman from Namibia was nonetheless arrested and questioned on her return, although she was released again after a while. One young man from Iran was arrested as he was leaving at Teheran airport. He was imprisoned and tortured and released only after three months of secret negotiations at the highest level and the payment of some ten thousands of dollars. I will never forget the evening at our home in Amsterdam when this young Iranian met old Stefan from Poland. The two of them talked for hours and then just sat silently next to each other for the rest of the evening. I have documented some of the statements from lesbians and gays around the world (van Dijk, 1998 and 2002).

Barry was too modest to mention that he was instrumental in organising two reading tours to the USA for Stefan T. Kosinski, including extended interviews at the Washington Holocaust Memorial Museum and the Shoah Foundation of Steven Spielberg in Los Angeles. Barry was also the driving force behind the Hungarian translation of *Damned Strong Love* while he was working in Budapest. Later, Barry and I travelled together to conduct teacher training seminars in eastern Europe. It was during those trips, which involved endless hours in trains and cold hotel rooms, when I felt the depth of his commitment to human rights of every human being. When he asked me to join him in working on this book I did not hesitate for a moment.

The book opens with a foreword by Archbishop emeritus Desmond Mpilo Tutu, the famous South African Nobel Peace Prize Laureate, who never accepted limiting human rights to only certain categories of people, even when living under the most horrible threats to his own life. His words set the inspirational tone for the rest of the book. Then Peter Dankmeijer from the Netherlands, who formed a global cooperation network on sexual diversity, places the chapters that follow into a global context. He argues that the concept of homophobia is linked to the way homosexuality is defined and experienced in the western world, which is the focus of this book. Outside the confines of the West the concept needs redefining.

The rest of the book is divided into three parts which focus on what can be done both within and beyond schools.

In the first part, *Challenging Homophobia in Primary and Secondary Schools* Renée DePalma and Mark Jennett from England share their thoughts about the obstacles and possibilities that exist at primary school level. They argue that too often discussions of homosexuality are avoided until secondary school. They make a strong case for addressing the matter much earlier and describe efforts to make an impact on younger age groups. Barry van Driel focuses on ways to address homophobia among Muslim youth in Europe who adhere to traditional views. Based on a larger European Union project on sexual diversity, Stefan Timmermanns reports on the need for education and counselling for LGBT-identified individuals in German schools.

In the second part, *Beyond schools: from support groups to constitutional rights to university settings* we explore the context of homophobia beyond schools and classrooms while always seeking out possible positive ways to support sexual diversity education. Jesus de Generelo from Spain shows how new political developments in Spain have made it possible to address homophobia in a traditionally Catholic and culturally conservative nation. Debbie Epstein and her colleagues look at how efforts to tackle homophobia in the UK compare with those made to tackle racism. They argue that anti-racist education has been largely accepted, but that homophobia among UK youth is largely ignored.

Dawn Betteridge and Lutz van Dijk report about the first steps being taken towards sexual diversity education in South Africa. Darren Lund discusses the creation of gay-straight alliances of learners and teachers in Canada and how various obstacles were overcome.

Michele Kahn analyses strategies to overcome homophobia in the conservative Christian setting of Texas in the USA. She shows how students can be challenged to confront the assumptions and stereo-types they hold about the GLBT (gay-lesbian-bisexual-transgender) community. Melinda L. de Jesus also looks at homophobia in the United States. She uses a university- based case study to show how she has addressed homophobia in an Asian-American context. Krzysztof Zablocki from Poland calls his contribution 'Surviving under Pressure', and shows what kinds of steps can be taken in a re-actionary Catholic environment.

The book concludes with **Examples of Best Practice**: a diverse collection of exciting, inspiring and sometimes controversial accounts of best practice in tackling homophobic attitudes. Authors of some of the earlier chapters have contributed to this section, suggesting their 'favourite' lesson plans, strategies and exercises. Some of these best practices and more can be found on the TANDIS (Tolerance and Non-Discrimination Information System) website of the Organisation for Democratic Institutions and Human Rights (ODIHR) which has reserved a special 'corner' for these (http://tandis.odihr.pl/?p= ki-ho).

We sincerely hope that our readers will feel encouraged to develop and try out their own best practices. It can be done... everywhere.

Lutz van Dijk and Barry van Driel
Cape Town and Brussels, April 2007

* * *

The editors and authors have agreed to donate their royalties to the LGBT-work of Amnesty International, London.

About the authors

Dawn Betteridge, born in Newcastle UK, came to South Africa with her parents as a baby in the 1970s. She studied architecture at the University of Port Elisabeth (Eastern Cape, South Africa), where she became a lesbian activist. Although she graduated successfully with an architectural degree, she has gone on to focus on human rights and LGBT issues. From 2001 – 2006 she was executive director of the Triangle Project (www.triangle.org.za), a Cape Town based non profit LGBT organisation. In 2007 she started working for the Schorer-Foundation in Amsterdam. d.betteridge@schorernet.nl

Peter Dankmeijer, born in Amsterdam, the Netherlands, was trained as a teacher but now works as senior consultant on gay and lesbian issues. He is director of Empowerment Lifestyle Services, a Dutch non-profit company which focuses on gay and lesbian emancipation in schools. In the Netherlands, Empowerment develops resources and implementation projects, advises authorities and NGOs and trains teachers and volunteer educators (www.empower-ls.com). One of his international activities is the management of the Global Alliance for LGBT Education (www.lgbt-education.info). info@empower-ls.com.

Lutz van Dijk, PhD, born in Berlin, Germany, worked as a teacher at special schools and teacher trainer at the University of Hamburg in Germany, before he joined the staff of the Anne Frank House in Amsterdam. Since 2001 he has been in Cape Town as a co-founder and executive co-director of HOKISA (Homes for Kids in South Africa, www.hokisa.co.za), a non-profit organisation caring for children and youth affected by HIV/AIDS. In 2003 he received the German *Rosa Courage Award* for his support of sexual minorities as a writer, historian and human rights activist. He also writes books for young readers like *Damned Strong Love* (a true story about the persecution of gays during Nazi times, 1995), *Stronger than the Storm* (a novel about teenage rape and HIV/AIDS in a South African township, 2000) and *The History of Love and Sex* (2007). lutzvandijk@iafrica.com

Barry van Driel, born in Glens Falls, New York, was educated at universities in the Netherlands and the United States. He holds a degree in the Psychology of Culture and Religion. He joined the staff of the Anne Frank House in 1992, where he is now international director for teacher training and curriculum development. He has been Editor in Chief of the international academic journal *Intercultural Education* http://www.tandf.co.uk/journals/titles/14675986. asp since 2000 and Secretary General of the International Association for Intercultural Education (www.iaie.org) since 2002. Barry is also senior education consultant to the Office for Democratic Institutions and Human Rights (ODIHR) in Warsaw. His books include *Variant Lifestyles* (with Bram Buunk, 1986) and most recently *Confronting Islamophobia in Educational Practice* (2005). barry@iaie.org.

Debbie Epstein, born in Pretoria, South Africa, is Professor of Education in the School of Social Sciences at Cardiff University. She has published widely on sexuality, gender, race and education and is currently working with colleagues on a book about gender and sexuality in South African schools in the context of the HIV/AIDS pandemic. Her books include: *Schooling Sexualities* (with Richard Johnson), *A Dangerous Knowing: sexuality, pedagogy and popular culture* (with James T. Sears) and *Border Patrols: Policing the Boundaries of Heterosexuality* (with Richard Johnson and Deborah Lynn Steinberg). She is co-editor of the journal *Gender and Education.* epsteind@Cardiff.ac.uk. Debbie's co-authors are: **Roger Hewitt**, who has conducted major ethnographnic projects in urban settings, including a notable ethnography and sociolinguistic analysis of black/white urban adolescent relations in south London and four important studies of racist violence; **Diana Leonard**, professor of the sociology of education and gender at the Institute of Education, University of London; **Melanie Mauthner** a social science lecturer at the Open University, and **Chris Watkins,** Reader in Education at the Institute of Education.

Jesús Generelo, born in Huesca, Spain, established the COGAM (Gay, Lesbian, Bisexual and Transexual Association of Madrid) Education Department, where he is the director. He is also a television producer. Under his guidance, COGAM has released several studies, including: *Familias de hecho: la realidad social de las familias formadas por gays, lesbianas y sus hijos, Homofobia en el Sistema Educativo* and *Adolescencia y sexualidades minoritarias: voces desde la exclusión*. He has published numerous pedagogical materials and gives workshops on sexual diversity in schools for teachers. In addition, he has written books such as *How to overcome homophobia* (Madrid, 2004), *Without complexes: a guide for LGTB teenagers* (Madrid, 2007), and the novel *Final de curso* (Barcelona, 2006). jgenerelo@ eresmas.net

Melinda Luisa de Jesús, born in Pennsylvania USA, is Associate Professor of Critical Studies at California College of the Arts in Oakland, California. Her research interests include Asian American culture, feminist/queer studies and critical pedagogy. She recently edited the first collection of Filipina/American feminist theory: *Pinay Power – Feminist Critical Theory* (New York, 2005). Her work has appeared in: *The Lion and the Unicorn; Meridians: Feminism, Race, Transnationalism; MELUS Journal; The Journal of Asian American Studies and Radical Teacher.* Melinda is an Aquarian and admits an obsession with Hello Kitty. mdejesus@cca.edu.

Mark Jennett is a trainer and writer specialising in work with schools, local authorities and others around diversity, sexual health, homophobia and bullying. His clients have included the General Teaching Council, Stonewall, NUT, NASUWT, Terrence Higgins Trust and the Greater London Authority and he is currently working as diversity trainer with the 'No Outsiders' project. He is the principle author of *Stand Up For Us*, a resource produced in conjunction with DfES and DH which offers support and guidance to schools on how to take a whole school approach to addressing homophobia, and edited *Sexual Exclusion – homophobia and health inequalities*, a review of health inequalities and social exclusion experienced by LGB people which was published by the Gay Men's Health Network.

Michele Malamud Kahn, born in Louisiana but raised in Guatemala, is an assistant professor of multicultural education at the University of Houston-Clear Lake. Her research and teaching interests focus on teacher beliefs, gender, and LGB issues in education. She is currently working on two projects, Life altering experiences and teacher identity and Gender ideology in teacher dress codes. Recent article: Conservative Christian teachers: Possible consequences for lesbian, gay, and bisexual youth, in: *Intercultural Education* 2006. michelemkahn@yahoo.com

Darren E. Lund, born in Canada, is an Associate Professor in the Faculty of Education at the University of Calgary where he teaches and researches issues around social justice activism in schools. He has published widely in antiracist education, and has been recognised for his social justice work with numerous awards and honours including a 2005 Killam Resident Fellowship, a 2005 Alberta Centennial Medal and the 2004 Educational Research Award from the Alberta Teachers' Association. A recent project is his on-line Diversity Toolkit: http://www.ucalgary.ca/~dtoolkit; dlund@ucalgary. ca

Renée DePalma, born in Trenton, NJ, received her PhD from the University of Delaware (USA), where she helped to develop and teach equality and diversity courses for preservice teachers. She is currently a Research Fellow at the University of Sunderland (UK) on an ESRC-funded project entitled 'No Outsiders: Researching approaches to sexualities equality in primary schools'. As senior researcher, she coordinates a team of teachers and re-search assistants conducting participatory action research projects in primary schools throughout the UK, with the goal of understanding and redressing im-plicit processes of heteronormativity and homophobia. rhayes@mundo-r.com

Stefan Timmermanns, PhD, born in Aachen, Germany, is an independent consultant. He was one of the initiators of SchLAu-NRW (www.schlau-nrw. de), an umbrella organisation of volunteer groups who go to schools to con-duct panel discussions with students in North Rhine-Westphalia. He was co-ordinator of the European TRIANGLE Project, which has developed a manual about combating homophobia in multicultural schools and counselling centres (www.diversity-in-europe.org). Since 2005, he has worked in a local Family Planning Organisation, giving sex education in schools. Stefan was originally trained as a secondary school teacher. He is member of the board of the German Association for Sex Education (www.gsp-ev.de) and the advisory board of the Global Alliance for LGBT Education (www.lgbt-education.info). Email: mail@timmermanns.eu.

Krzysztof Zablocki, born in Warsaw, Poland, has an MA degree in English literature and is currently teaching English and American Culture at Warsaw University. He also works as a freelance translator. He has translated from English and French into Polish authors including Jean Genet, Edmund White, Emily Dickinson and Paul Auster and has published several essays on English and French literature. He does volunteer work at Lambda Warszawa: www. lambda.org.pl; k.zablocki@uw.edu.pl

Part 1
Challenging homophobia in primary and secondary schools

1

Starting global collaboration in education about sexual diversity

Peter Dankmeijer

This chapter describes some of the key findings from a needs assessment conducted for the Global Alliance for LGBT Education (www.lgbt-education.info) and reflects on regional differences that can either limit or facilitate transnational collaboration. Cultural and political settings strongly influence situational definitions, goals and the development of appropriate educational methods. The chapter moves on to sum up the various interpretations of homophobia and sexual diversity discrimination, since defining what we are combating or promoting is crucial for common understanding and collaboration. It concludes that collaboration is possible when heteronormativity is taken as the underlying concept to be challenged and when people are able to transcend cultural views. International exchange can be helpful in gaining an enhanced understanding of what social exclusion really is and how it can be effectively combated.

A needs assessment

In 1998, Amnesty International and HIVOS[1] organised the first global workshop on education against homophobia. The main recommendation of this workshop was to create a global network for exchange and to raise the quality of work being done. During the years 2003-2005, I initiated an assessment of views on education about lesbian, gay, bisexual, transgender (LGBT) issues and the need to create a network.

The needs assessment involved two hour long interviews with a variety of respondents who came from a diversity of backgrounds: voluntary or professional educators working specifically on gay or lesbian issues, transgender activists, AIDS prevention workers, researchers, family planning and sex education trainers, government officials and representatives from other sectors such as lawyers and police officers. What they all had in common was an interest in education about LGBT issues. The interviews took place between 2003 and 2006 in Italy, Finland, Sweden, France, the UK, Austria, India, Thailand, South Africa, Namibia, Australia, Mexico, Colombia, Brazil, Peru, Argentina and the USA. This chapter is based on the outcomes of about 60 interviews and a range of additional information which was collected both earlier and in response to the needs assessment. This chapter focuses exclusively on the school sector.

Regional differences
This section provides an overview of some regional differences.

The western world: sexual identity strategies
In Europe and in North America sexual orientation identities are central in combating discrimination against those with homosexual, bisexual and lesbian feelings. Assuming an identity and pointing at the norm of heterosexuality as the dominant system of oppression is central to 'the struggle' in those parts of the world. Often there are separate movements of self-identified gays and lesbians. The gay movement focuses on sexual liberation and acceptance of homosexual identities while the lesbian movement focuses on gender rights and on combating the heterosexual norm. The gay movement is usually more outspoken than the lesbian movement. One aspect of this male dominance is that the western gay movement usually speaks of 'combating homophobia' because its implicit focus is on fighting discrimination. This has been an effective approach in the last two decades. The European Union has adopted guidelines against discrimination in employment, based on seven grounds

4

including sexual orientation. More needs to be done: discrimination in other areas like education, housing and services is only prohibited on the grounds of gender, race and perhaps disability.

The dominance of the anti-homophobia model translates itself into a particular method of education which is typical in Western Europe and some parts of Canada and the US: the Gay Panel Discussion[2]. Lesbian and gay volunteer groups ask schools to invite them for a panel discussion. The structure of these panel discussions may vary. There seem to be three models, often blended into one programme:

- introduction of the gay/lesbian group and an invitation to gay and lesbian youth to join

- open question time – any question is allowed

- telling a personal story – often with a focus on coming out.

This model is popular in Europe because coming out is the main personal strategy for emancipation. Students tend to have great curiosity about how others construct their identities, especially in situations where identities may be discredited and when questions about sex are allowed. The method seems especially effective when questions are answered and stories are told in a personal and authentic way.

In addition to Gay Panel Discussions, which focus on the personal attitudes of students, there is an increasing number of projects which focus more on improving school policies and on preventing homophobic behaviour. Like the Panel Discussions, most of these projects focus on sexual identity strategies. Gay and lesbian associations often collaborate with trade unions to make schools safer for gays and lesbians. The two main aims are to stop discriminatory or marginalising behaviour and to support the coming out of gay and lesbian teachers and students. A range of interventions have been developed for these purposes: school policy documents, disciplinary and pedagogical guidelines, training, specific and integrated attention to gay and lesbian issues in the curriculum and gay and lesbian student counselling.

These projects seek to be effective by combining a wide range of methods with a focus on behaviour. However, it is often difficult to implement them successfully because schools are rarely willing to put energy into what they see as a minority problem of little significance.

Middle and Eastern Europe: strategy of equal treatment

The picture in middle and eastern Europe looks entirely different: a return to religion and conservative nationalism after the fall of Communism has created a new, unsafe context for LGBT people (see the chapter by Krzysztof Zablocki). Although a range of countries pledged allegiance to 'European' standards of equal treatment in order to enter the European Union, in practice the human rights of LGBT people are barely respected. Nevertheless, a range of LGBT organisations has been created during the last decade. After a phase of basic capacity building, these organisations are now starting to focus on external projects, ranging from pride marches and cultural festivals to HIV prevention and educational projects. Visibility projects like pride marches, festivals and poster campaigns are seen as stepping stones to more advanced educational methods in formal settings. It is too early to say which direction projects focused at schools will take. Most school systems in eastern Europe are centralised and government authorities are not yet open to extending human rights or sex education to LGBT issues. The extreme homophobic attitudes of local populations make it unlikely that the Panel Discussion model will be exported to the east.

Gay-straight alliances in the USA

In the USA the model of gay-straight alliances (GSAs) has taken root. GSAs are high school student clubs which provide a safe space for LGBT students and sometimes play a role in extra-curricular education and in advocacy for safer school policies. The participants in GSAs are both LGBT and heterosexual: research has shown that the majority of the participants are heterosexual girls. On a national level the Gay, Lesbian, Straight Education Network (GLSEN) supports local GSAs with resources and by facilitating exchange.

GSAs operate in the context of a school club culture. Most US students take part in one or more extra-curricular school clubs, which are usually supported and funded by the school. There may be sports clubs or hobby clubs, but a range of the clubs are identity based, such as racial or cultural identity related clubs. Although GSAs are not strictly identity based, their purpose is to promote tolerance towards identity politics. The school club system is specific to the USA which, in addition to the focus on identity politics, may explain why the GSA model has not spread much outside the USA.

The diversity of cultures, ethnic and religious groups in the USA is gradually having a larger impact on the LGBT and diversity movements. In so-called 'rainbow' curricula, LGBT issues are increasingly being recognised and GLSEN has been collaborating with specific groups, for example by allying with the Metropolitan Community Church and by translating GSA manuals into Spanish.

Latin America: fluid sexualities

For most Latin Americans it is hardly relevant to talk about sexual orientation in the context of identity. For Latin Americans two concepts are much more important: machismo and sexualities.

Heteronormativity is important to Latin America. Sex role patterns are extremely pronounced: the dynamic between macho men and feminine women is crucial. Social order is largely organised around these gender roles. In this social model women should have a submissive position to macho men and people who display non-heterosexual feelings or atypical gender behaviour are discredited. At the same time sexuality and erotic play remain an important means of communication and of defining power and pleasure. Part of this is the phenomenon of 'travestis', people who in various ways cross gender roles. This may be by cross dressing, by using hormones and props or by full surgery but there is no single scenario of transsexuality. Within the limits of the heteronormative context, there is plenty of space for experimentation and pleasure which is not heterosexual or limited to typical gender roles. Some respondents refer to this as having 'fluid sexualities'.

Most Latin American nations have a history of dictatorships as well as movements against such oppression. The dictatorships tended to use conservative gender and family role patterns to control the population. This kept women in a powerless position and tied men to the non-political maintenance of their family. In this context any behaviour not focused on the family could be seen as a threat to the security of the state. However, with the fall of dictatorships civil societies started to develop. The main aims of the Latin American civil society movement have been to promote a sense of individual empowerment and space for self-expression. The LGBT organisations are often able to collaborate with a wider civil rights movement to achieve such aims.

This situation has several consequences for the aims and content of education about sexual diversity in Latin America. Firstly, a single focus on homophobia would not be appropriate in cultures where almost nobody is 'homo' but where fluid sexualities are common practice. Second, the connection of the LGBT movement to the wider civil rights movement makes it logical to focus on personal empowerment and rights to self-expression. In practice these needs crystallise in collaboration on sex education programmes with explicit components on sexual rights and sexual diversity.

An example of this is the sex education programme for secondary schools, developed by the Brazilian LGBT organisation *Dignidade* (in Curitiba, capital of the Brazilian State of Parana) in collaboration with the city-funded sex education organisation CEPAC. This program is a course consisting of five modules. The first module is about self-awareness and empowerment. The course goes on to discuss sexuality, stressing personal choices, mutual respect and the context of masculinity and femininity. At the end of the course, when students have got used to talking openly and respectfully about sex and personal differences, sexual diversity is picked up as yet another aspect of diversity.

Other examples can be found in the plans of both the city of Bogotá and the Ministry of Education of Colombia. In Colombia the civil war has stressed tolerance to its limits. The progressive part of the peace movement focuses not just on 'ending the war', but on empowering citizens to ask for and defend their civil rights, including women's and sexual rights. Progressive authorities now embark on programmes in schools which give explicit attention to a range of diversities, allying with civil society (including the LGBT organisation Colombia Diversa) on programme development. The Mayor of Bogotá appointed a new city department of ten professionals entirely devoted to supporting schools with a diversity policy. 'Diversity' here refers not only to gender or sexual orientation but to intellectual capabilities, handicaps, indigenous groups and 'displaced persons' (a euphemism for farmers who had to flee the countryside to cities because of the civil war) as well.

These developments are still in their early stages but there is a vigorous eagerness to learn about good practice and to start implementing programmes.

Asia: hierarchical respect

In Asia most countries have cultures with long historical roots and social arrangements that are relatively rigid. One of the most important features of these societies is the importance of respect, especially for people who are higher in the hierarchy. India, with its caste system, is perhaps the most profound example of this. But other Asian cultures also have embedded status differences and respect in their languages and social patterns, such as detailed norms regarding how to greet each other. Most of these established social systems are organised in a heteronormative way. People who display non-heterosexual feelings or atypical gender behaviour can fall into two categories: either they commit themselves to a social group which accepts and defines their behaviour within a traditional (low status) section of society, or they become complete outcasts. In most Asian countries there are groups of transsexuals who have a traditional way of existence but remain fundamentally part of the lower strata of society.

In Asia, sexuality is traditionally not a taboo, although there are rules and restrictions connected to the social hierarchy. Conservative Asian governments that pretend to restore 'original Asian culture', usually still adopt negative colonial views on sexuality. Prescribed gender roles are important too, but they are not acted out as they are in Latin America. A public show of eroticism is largely taboo – except for Japan where the state religion of Shintoism created tolerance of all expressions of sexuality of a holy nature.

9

In many countries arranged marriages are traditional and sexuality is supposed to be a reproductive act within marriage. Having children confers status on married women. Several of my Indian respondents told me that many women refuse to have sex with their husband after they have had enough children to guarantee good social status. They claimed that this is part of the reason for high levels of incest, rape and homosexual behaviour by men.

Sex and human rights education are fairly unknown in most parts of Asia. Many state authorities claim that the human rights framework and open discussion of sexuality are alien to Asian culture and make efforts to exclude it from the school curricula. A range of Asian countries have stated that the human rights framework is alien to Asia because it stresses individual freedoms. Furthermore, they insist that open discussion of sexuality and especially of homosexualities is also alien. They contend that Asian values focus on respect, but that these are local, not codified and based in culture. They neglect to mention that these 'respectful' attitudes are rooted in cultural systems which maintain social inequality and actually foster disrespect for people who are lower on the social ladder. With the slow emergence of public influence on governments, such issues have become more important and more political. Disempowered communities gradually see opportunities to improve their situation by forging coalitions with communities with similar demands. LGBT groups are often able to ally with women's groups, development NGOs, AIDS service organisations, law reform movements and environmental groups which give them access to mainstream policies and institutions, be it often slightly covert. The AIDS pandemic has had growing impact on Asia too, especially in social networks where people have secret male to male contact or have to resort to prostitution to survive. This creates a need for prevention and sex education. Asian authorities find this need difficult to cope with.

Because of the inability of most Asian authorities to deal with the range of demands relating to rights and sex education, a range of grass roots initiatives have emerged, with or without tacit tolerance of the authorities. On one hand, we have the emergence of a range of sex education programmes dealing with AIDS, birth control and gender roles. Sometimes it is possible to integrate respect towards people with a non-heteronormative gender identity or sexual contacts in these programmes. An example of this is the sex education programme in a high school in Bangalore, which focused on self-esteem and respect between genders. In its wake attention was devoted to 'all people with different lifestyles', including *hijras* – the locally visible form of transgenderism/same sex relationships. Students were not only educated, but coached to do outreach education about these issues in their home communities as well. Although the programme was called a 'sex education programme', sexuality itself was not discussed explicitly. The programme focused more on the social context of sexuality.

On the other hand, there are a range of outreach activities in the context of AIDS prevention. The NAZ Foundation conducts important work in this area. Although their interventions are not based on outreach to people who label themselves based on same sex preference, considerable attention is devoted to reaching out and supporting communities and networks of at risk populations, like varying cultural forms of transgenders, prostitutes and truck drivers who have same sex contacts. The educational approach does not limit itself to condom use but encompasses self-esteem, empowerment and human rights. The educational strategy includes creating structural conditions to improve the situation, like advocacy for legal reform – in India to abolish the sodomy law and relax the persecution of prostitutes – training for health professionals and creating health centres for people with same sex contacts.

Due to the lack of support from local authorities, most of these programmes rely on international funding. Only a minority of mainly European funded programmes can give balanced attention to prostitution and same sex contacts. Much of the funding comes from the USA and this means that it is difficult to deal with human rights and sexualities that do not conform to fundamentalist Christian values.

Australia: first steps
The needs assessment in Australia was mostly limited to Melbourne and the rural areas to the north. It is difficult to assess whether or not the impressions from these interviews reflect the situation in Aus-

tralia as a whole since there seems to be no national exchange of experiences around LGBT strategies in this country. It appears that education about sexual diversity has not taken hold in Australian schools although there are some references to gay and lesbian issues in the sex education curricula which are implemented at the state level.

One outstanding example of a LGBT specific intervention is the Pride and Prejudice (http://www.prideandprejudice.com.au/) programme. This is a six-week secondary school programme developed by Daniel Witthaus, a youth worker who received severe homophobic comments from the boys he worked with. He developed a draft programme to deal with these attitudes and was quickly asked to make it more widely available and to provide teacher training. Deakin University's Psychology department researched the programme and found that it significantly changed students' attitudes towards gay men and lesbians.The programme is currently spreading across several Australian states and Witthaus is working full-time to promote it.

Africa: fierce resistance
In Africa education about LGBT issues in mainstream institutions remains largely unexplored. In most African countries both authorities and populations fiercely oppose any sexual diversity. The cultural and historical existence of same sex relationships is denied or labelled as 'imported western decadence'. Some countries even legally forbid any hint of same sex attraction. This situation makes education difficult. The only two exceptions are South Africa and Namibia.

South Africa has undergone a wave of progressive policies since the abolition of apartheid, legally combating all forms of discrimination. However, personal attitudes do not change just because laws change (see the chapter by Dawn Betteridge and Lutz van Dijk). A majority of the South African population still holds negative attitudes towards same sex relationships. Local LGBT groups have recently started to experiment with educational interventions, such as publishing personal life stories, organising panel discussions in schools and the creation of a teacher training programme. All these still seem to be in their early stages. In Namibia there is one main LGBT organisation: the Rainbow Project. This organisation has a range of projects which mainly focus on capacity building of local LGBT populations. AIDS prevention is one of the priorities and educational methods have been developed for LGBT individuals and also for nurses. A project targeting schools is on its way but will need to focus on general human rights rather than just LGBT issues in order to placate the authorities.

In some North African countries, HIV prevention targets gay prostitutes and young people but the issue of sexual contacts and human rights is approached indirectly and cautiously.

One of the main priorities on the African continent is to make the general population and the authorities aware that same sex relationships are indigenous to Africa and not a threat to national security or 'African masculinity'. A certain visibility of LGBT issues will be necessary to attain that goal but this kind of visibility needs to be balanced with more acceptance by local populations and authorities. This will be a slow and careful process, starting with basic capacity building by local LGBT people themselves. Storytelling is an important tool for communication and education in Africa. The Johannesburg-based project Behind The Mask (http://www.mask.org.za) offers comprehensive information on sexual diversity in African local situations and uses hundreds of personal stories in its work. In addition a group called All African Rights Initiative recently started to promote and support these local strategies. A few years ago the Coalition of African Lesbians started to support the capacity building and visibility of women.

The Arab World: acceptability in the face of Islam

Similar fierce resistance can be found in Arab countries and countries where Sharia (Islamic law) is part of the legal system. Here the basis for rejection of sexual diversity is the Qu'ran and its teachings. Public education about LGBT issues is not possible in most of these countries, especially in contexts where the words of the Qu'ran are taken literally.

Nonetheless, the last decade has seen some significant new voices. The US-based LGBT organisation Al-Fatiha (http://www.al-fatiha. org) focuses on the capacity building of gay Muslims. An important aspect of this is the development of novel Qu'ran interpretations, which allow some space for LGBT individuals to carve out an identity. We find these for instance in the Netherlands (Yoesuf: http://www.yoesuf.nl), Belgium (Merhaba: http://www.merhaba. be), Germany (The Miles Project: http://www.berlin.lsvd.de/cms/ index.php?option=com_content&task=view&id=22&Itemid=64) and the UK (Al-bab: http://www.al-bab.com/; Safra Project: http:// www.safraproject.org (lesbian)).

Muslim gay and lesbian activists have joined the debate and are looking for models to create more acceptance of sexual diversity. This needs to be done before they can embark on educational efforts. One debate is whether gay and lesbian Muslims should focus on justification of sexual diversity through Qu'ran-based interpretations or through appeals to cultural tolerance. Another debate is about whether same sex behaviour or feelings can be justified at all. After much recent debate, some consensus seems to be emerging: to focus on respect and to rely on Qu'ranic references that only Allah is allowed to judge people.

In Europe and in some isolated cases like Azerbaijan, workshops are given to health professionals, teachers and secondary school students on respect towards people who have same sex feelings. In these workshops the difference between the reality of human emotions and behaviours and the guidelines associated with the Qu'ran and cultural pressure are central concerns. See Barry van Driel's chapter for further discussion of some of these issues.

Different interpretations of LGBT exclusion

Regional situations lead to different interpretations and labelling of sexual diversity. These are major factors to consider when teaching about 'homophobia'. This section is devoted to the relevance of these interpretations.

It is clear that concepts such as 'gay and lesbian' or 'homosexual' are western and limited to sexual orientation as a social identity. The use of these words can be counterproductive and unacceptable in many parts of the world. The same goes for the concept of homophobia, used in the title of this book. This concept has received some criticism for being scientifically incorrect, but the word homophobia is still used by activists and educators because it sounds clear and challenging. In education using words like gay, lesbian, homosexual and homophobia may lead to the exclusion of transgender issues and imply an artificial binary between homosexual and heterosexual relationships. Furthermore, it may distract attention from heteronormativity, which is what creates social exclusion and discrimination. Some groups in the west may want to reconsider to what extent teaching about 'homosexual identity' or 'against homophobia' is effective in modifying heteronormative attitudes and behaviour.

Attempts have been made to be more inclusive and various acronyms are used: GLBT (gay, lesbian, bisexual, transgender), LGBT, TLGB, and LGBTQI (lesbian, gay, bisexual, transgender, questioning or queer, intersex). The order of the letters is never accidental: they signify the priority organisations give to combat discrimination of the most vulnerable groups. The disadvantage of all these attempts is that they still categorise.

We also see attempts to be even more inclusive by using the concept of 'sexual minorities'. However, some respondents say that this has the disadvantage of putting people in a victim role and gives the false impression that heterosexually identified people cannot engage in homosexual encounters. This is especially a problem in parts of the world where large percentages of the (male) population engage in same sex behaviour. These categorising definitions all limit the scope of education because labelling implies a focus on identity politics. This supports self-awareness and may be useful to build the personal capacity of disenfranchised people but it limits the opportunities to educate heterosexuals about their stake in heteronormative systems.

The most inclusive concept is 'sexual diversity'. It implies recognition of a continuum of feelings and identities and integrates heterosexual behaviour. However, the disadvantage is that it is rather

15

vague; heterosexuals may not know what the word refers to. In educational practice, using the concept of sexual diversity as a starting point makes it logical not to focus on identities but on sex education in general. This provides many opportunities but carries the risk that such a wide focus will obstruct or dilute the effort to combat specific forms of discrimination.

The Global Alliance for LGBT Education settled on its name to avoid the ambiguity of the more correct term of sexual diversity and to make the issues it deals with visible in a positive and non-confrontational way.

Conclusions

The intensity and type of resistance towards sexual diversity point to the urgent need to collaborate on a global level. Each LGBT or mainstream organisation makes choices about how to deal with such local cultural heteronormative resistance. There are many similarities in how they modify discriminatory attitudes and behaviour at classroom level but the strategic way of implementing programmes is usually more culturally and regionally specific. Collaboration at global level will depend on how a balance can be struck between these similarities and differences.

Global differences in interpretations of homophobia seem to be so substantial that it may be hard to agree on common grounds and to exchange learning experiences. With increasing globalisation and migration this becomes even more relevant: global differences may become visible in every classroom. The growing diversity in this world needs new methods of dealing with diversity. For LGBT people, it is clear that diversity education should not just focus on celebrating – cultural or other – differences but on the common ground of self-esteem, social competence, tolerance and respect.

Clearly, heteronormativity is still a common factor across cultures. Identities, concepts of sexuality and educational strategies develop within specific cultural contexts but the underlying mechanism of social exclusion is always heteronormativity. Heteronormative systems offer individuals and state authorities a sense of stability and safety. Both individual identities and cultural authorities rely on rigid gender and sexual norms to maintain control and security. This stability is threatened by deviant behaviour which is thought to challenge the system and personal heteronormative identities. Collaboration at global level should therefore focus on debate and experimentation on how to modify heteronormative systems and behaviour.

Internationally an unholy alliance of fundamentalist Muslim and Christian movements has been emerging. These movements find each other in their fear of change and common prohibitions on sexual liberty found in the Bible and the Qu'ran. Their strategy relies on imposing rigid norms and authoritarian control on citizens. However, the more cramped these attempts to control and to limit diversity are, the more they are challenged, even in their own communities. Almost invisible for outsiders, they struggle with their own internal dilemmas.

From the needs assessment it becomes clear that several models of intervention have been developed to combat discrimination. However, in many cases educational methods focus on the most obvious representations of discrimination, which are cultural and regional, rather than on the underlying variable of heteronormativity. For example, the Gay Panel Discussion focuses more on explaining homosexual identity than on challenging heteronormativity. Some interventions in the Global South focus on 'respect' within existing cultural frameworks rather than aiming to modify those frameworks. In a way this is understandable. Aims and methods develop within specific cultural contexts and it is difficult to transcend those limits when you are not aware of other possibilities. International collaboration and exchange would be helpful to achieve an enhanced understanding of social exclusion and how it can be challenged through education.

The Global Alliance for LGBT Education is embarking on an internet platform for exchange and collaboration, as well as a number of pilot projects which focus on a range of institutions such as the media, health services and the police force. Although schools in the global south are difficult to access, the Alliance has decided that a specific focus on school strategies and teacher training must be one of the first priorities. A working group for teacher training was created and an active collection of good practices started towards the end of 2007. The Alliance invites all concerned to join the learning community it provides and to add to the database of resources.

Notes

1 'Humanistisch Instituut voor Ontwikkeling Samenwerking': Humanist Institute for Development Collaboration, a Dutch donor focusing on supporting developing countries. HIVOS was the first Dutch development organisation in the Netherlands to take LGBT issues as a priority.

2 See for example: Gay Panel Discussions in the Netherlands: http://www.empower-ls.com/nl/schoolondersteuning/voorlichtingsgroepen; in Germany: http://www.schlau-nrw.de/; Canada: http://www.gris.ca/

2

Deconstructing heteronormativity in primary schools in England: cultural approaches to a cultural phenomenon

Renée DePalma and Mark Jennett

Despite its importance in terms of pupil, teacher and community well-being, sexualities equality[1] remains the one area of inclusion which is still not addressed in schools, yet this pressing human rights issue is recognised in the UK by the Department for Education and Skills (DfES), the Office for Standards in Education (Ofsted) and the General Teaching Council for England (GTC). The urgent need to tackle this issue is demonstrated by abundant evidence of the prevalence of homophobia in schools (MacGillivray, 2004) and of the reality that heteronormativity is maintained in schools through both active and passive means (Epstein, O'Flynn and Telford, 2003).

When school-based homophobia is described in popular media or academic literature it is usually in the context of secondary school or post-secondary school. Sexualities equality, if addressed at all, is rarely addressed at primary level. Nevertheless, homophobia is a cultural phenomenon which can only be challenged by promoting the equality of lesbian, gay, bisexual and transgender people as part of a whole school ethos that celebrates diversity and challenges inequities of all kinds. The institutional culture of school as a whole must be transformed and this must begin at the beginning when children first walk through the school gate.

In this chapter we will situate homophobia as a cultural phenomenon, describe some of the reasons that inhibit teachers from addressing sexualities equality in primary schools and provide some information and resources to support teachers in this endeavour. Finally, we will describe the No Outsiders project, where 15 primary teachers throughout the UK are collaborating to promote LGBT equalities in their schools and classrooms.

Homophobia as a cultural process

Homophobia tends to be represented in the popular media in terms of homophobic bullying, focusing on isolated acts committed by certain types of people who are bullies against others who are victims. Drawing upon our own research over the past two years in the UK, as well as the research of others, we understand homophobia as the systemic and purposeful social policing of hegemonic masculinity. Violence against perceived homosexuals is a means of gender construction and simultaneously a developmental, communicative and social act. Recalling Crawford's (1993) understanding of gender as a verb rather than a noun and also Butler's description of the performativity of gender and sexuality (Butler, 1999), we argue that gender and sexuality are purposefully enacted rather than passively experienced. These performances are public and communicative, and can reinforce inequalities around socially mediated understandings of desirability and power. This implies that reducing homophobic abuse is more likely to occur through systematic and proactive social change than through simply preventing or reducing particular acts of violence. It also implies that a culture of homophobia does not emerge overnight or sometime during the summer between Year 6 and Year 7.

A needs assessment commissioned in the UK by the National Healthy Schools Programme (formerly the National Healthy School Standard – NHSS) into the views of school staff, pupils aged 7-18 and LGB young people revealed a pattern of habitual and purposeful homophobic abuse, coupled with ambivalent school response in primary as well as secondary schools:

■ The predominance of name-calling and the use of 'gay' as a term of abuse in primary schools were not seen as homophobic. Pupils felt that teachers did not consider these incidents to be significant, since they did not challenge them, and this was thought to be acceptable. Teachers confirmed that pupils, mainly boys, commonly used homophobic language

'It's mainly done jokey if you dislike people – everyone gets called gay at times' (Key Stage 2 pupil)

'They wouldn't say it if you were [actually] gay. They probably wouldn't even talk to you' (Key Stage 2 pupil)

■ Key Stage 3 and 4 pupils thought that schools did not take homophobic bullying as seriously as racist bullying. Some believed that schools denied having any LGB pupils and that some teachers were openly homophobic. They felt that LGB pupils would be victimised both verbally and physically, although this would happen less if the person were popular or older

■ Pupils felt that classmates with LGB parents would themselves become the target of homophobia[2].

In a recent controversial statement, responding to Radio 1 broadcaster Chris Moyles' description of a ring tone as 'gay', the BBC Board of Governors asserted that 'the word 'gay' now means 'rubbish' in modern playground-speak and need not be offensive to homosexuals' (Sherwin, 2006). This statement implies that children have ceased to understand the word as an insult that might be offensive to people as well as telephones and other inanimate objects. Nevertheless, a survey recently conducted among some 1,200 primary and secondary children in the UK by the charity Beatbullying, revealed that over three quarters of primary school-aged respondents identified the use of the word 'gay' as a way of attacking or making fun of someone. Surprisingly, the figure for secondary age respondents was only 40 per cent (personal communication John Quinn, Development Director, Beatbullying, 10 October 2006)[3]. What the BBC Board of Governors' response failed to address is that children with lesbian or gay parents, family members or friends, and children who themselves may come to identify as gay, are constantly barraged by the message that 'gay' is synonymous with ineptitude, undesirability and isolation. The National Union of Teachers (NUT) reports that children as young as three are using homophobic language, and that teachers need to learn how to affirm gay and lesbian relationships (Legg, 2006).

Childline, a child protection helpline run by the National Society for Prevention of Cruelty to Children (NSPCC), reports that 60 per cent of the young people who called to talk about sexual orientation, homophobia or homophobic bullying were 12 to 15, and 6 per cent were 11 or under. Their report includes quotes from an 11 year-old boy who declared that he was happy to be gay despite tormentors kicking him and calling him 'batty boy', a 10 year-old boy who was being called 'poo-boy'; an 11 year-old girl who was afraid to report to her teacher that she was being called 'dyke' and 'lemon'; a 10 year-old boy who reported that children were kicking him and calling him 'poofter' on the playground, but teachers did not believe him; and an 11 year-old girl whose teacher suggested she just keep away from the children who were calling her a 'fat lesbian' (NSPCC, 2006). These incidents reveal not only the range of homophobic abuse experienced by primary school-aged children but also the eerily unresponsive culture of the schools. These children are not describing isolated events that evoke an immediate and clear response from the school and teachers' uncertainty about how or even whether to respond reproduces rather than challenges homophobia.

It is over-simplistic to assume that the use of these homophobic taunts such as 'gay', 'poofter', and 'fat lesbian', even among young children, is divorced from the sexual and gender connotations they carry. In the Childline examples these children seemed all too painfully aware that these terms called into question not only their sexuality but also their femininity or masculinity. In popular culture sexual orientation is related to particular gender-associated behaviours and transgendered people are often associated with homosexuality and exaggerated masculinities and femininities, regardless of the diverse lived experiences of lesbian, gay, bisexual and trans-gendered people. Butler (1999) refers to the heterosexual matrix of sex-gender-sexuality which defines certain oppressed, silenced and marginalised sexual and gendered ways of being against a network of intersecting normative ways of performing sexuality and gender.

This understanding of homophobia and heteronormativity as purposeful hegemonic cultural forces, enacted through discourses that range from violence to silence, calls for a policy of proactive cultural change in primary schools. It means questioning the assumptions underpinning heteronormativity, not only in terms of what is said and done but also in terms of what is left out of the official discourse.

What stops teachers from addressing sexualities equality in the primary school?

DePalma and Atkinson's (2006a) interviews with lesbian, gay and straight primary teachers and teacher-trainees in the UK point to widespread under-estimation of the prevalence and significance of homophobia in schools. This seems to be partly due to the relative invisibility of LGBT teachers and parents. For example, out of twenty gay and lesbian teachers in this study only one gay man had come out to his pupils. While most teachers cited fear of reprisals from parents if they addressed sexualities equality in the classroom, not a single teacher suggested that LGBT parents – or any straight parents – might wish them to do so. Only a handful of gay and lesbian parents were identified by teachers, and these were often reluctant to be openly identified within the broader school community.

There is also reluctance among teachers to address sexualities equality in the primary years where an implicit conceptual link between sexual orientation and sexual activity has led teachers to avoid addressing same sex relationships in discussions of family, friendship, self or growing up, despite the fact that many children in their care have some connection, through family or friends, to non-heterosexual relationships and some are likely to identify in later life as lesbian, gay, bisexual or transgendered. Sears (1999) has pointed out the tendency to automatically associate sexual identity with sexual acts, which is borne out by our recent research into attitudes toward incorporating sexualities equality into primary schools.

This hyper-sexualisation of gay and lesbian sexualities clashes strongly with the widespread myth in primary schools of the asexual and naïve child. One contributor to an online discussion board evokes a simpler time from their childhood when knowledge of the existence of (hyper-sexualised) gay and lesbian people would have been dangerous information:

> Can anyone reflect back on how naïve and innocent you all were in primary school, even in secondary school, how would you have coped, what ideas would you have formed knowing such information? (see DePalma and Atkinson, 2006b for further analysis of this discussion)

However, these popular adult assumptions about the sexual ignorance of children have been challenged by research, including some primary classroom ethnographies that have explored the ways in which children's awareness of sexuality interacts with adults' discomfort and denial of it (Renold, 2005; Thorne, 1993). In a recent YWCA study young lesbians reported that the age when they first knew of their sexuality ranged from 6 to 12 years and that the average gap between young women realising they were lesbians and first telling someone about it was three years (YWCA England and Wales). This suggests that some children will be aware of their gay and lesbian identities long before secondary school. Even more striking is the three year gap between self-realisation and disclosure, a long silence during which the pervasive heteronormativity of primary and secondary schools is relentlessly at work.

In addition, the shadow of Section 28 of the 1988 Local Government Act has acted as a powerful constraint to those who might have wanted to address sexualities equality. Section 28 stated that a local authority shall not 'promote the teaching in any maintained school of the acceptability of homosexuality as a pretended family relationship'. It was repealed in 2003 (2000 in Scotland) and did not actually apply directly to classroom teachers, but some teachers still suspect that it prohibits them from even speaking of lesbian, gay and bisexual people in the classroom (DePalma and Atkinson, 2006a). It has even mobilised latent homophobia among some teachers (Ellis and High, 2004). Certainly the myth of the continuing viability of Section 28 is fuelled by the general atmosphere of fear and confusion around sexualities that pervades primary schools.

Primary teachers also cite fundamentalist religious groups as a strong inhibiting factor, describing fears of invoking retribution from committed Christians and fundamental Muslims, who are themselves minorities in British society (DePalma and Atkinson, 2006a). While other equalities issues such as race and disability continue to struggle with societal responses ranging from prejudice and majority outrage to apathy, sexualities equality is unique in being perceived as legitimately against someone's religion.

It is important to realise that this distinction begins to break down when we consider certain religious arguments for oppression, such as slavery in the US (Haynes, 2002) and the persecution of Jews in Europe (Dawidowicz, 1975). This is not to dismiss religious concerns but to suggest that it may be necessary to negotiate the boundaries when respecting one group's freedoms might mean limiting the freedoms of another (Okin *et al*, 1999). There may be no simple win-win situation but steps have been taken to reach beyond simple notions of shared commitments to universal equality to the rather messy push and pull of negotiation.

In the US, for example, the Gay, Lesbian, and Straight Education Network (GLSEN) and the Christian Educators Association International have collaborated in creating a plan for addressing LGBT issues in classrooms (First Amendment Center, 2006). While the report does not recommend specific practice or policy, the collaboration itself is a significant step toward recognising both the necessity and the difficulty of such work:

> Even finding the right terminology to discuss these differences that neither side will see as problematic can prove extremely difficult. One student's call for toleration is perceived by another student as a challenge to deeply held convictions. (First Amendment Center, 2006, p2)

Although homosexuality is sometimes referred to as a lifestyle, it is actually a fundamental aspect of personal identity. While teachers may be tempted to avoid the issue, especially in the light of pressures from some religious groups to consider gay, lesbian, bisexual and transgendered identities as unfortunate choices that can be changed or at least concealed, the reality is that freedom of sexuality is protected by law in the UK in much the same way as race, gender and disability. In a documentary film about addressing lesbian and gay equalities in American elementary schools (Chasnoff, 1996) one elementary school principal explains that she tells fundamentalist Christian parents that if they want her to defend their right to religious freedom they must allow her to promote lesbian and gay equality in her school. The reality is complex as teachers and parents negotiate this intersection of religious freedom and lesbian and gay rights on a case by case basis, but this principal has taken the important step of publicly recognising sexualities equality as a legitimate social justice issue.

There is much diversity within religious groups. Despite the fact that the most extreme right wing views seem to be heard the loudest, there are other religious discourses of love and acceptance that support LGBT equality. Michael Apple (2006) asks 'How can we bring religious discourse away from the right to become allies rather than have disdain for religion?'. Teachers might lose sight of the potential for religious allies. One gay primary teacher in DePalma and Atkinson's study was shocked when his committed Christian head told him about gay Christian groups and another was pleasantly surprised that Muslim parents on his Board of Governors supported him in coming out to his pupils (2006a). The following list of websites illustrates the diversity of religious support for LGBT people:

http://www.eflgc.org.uk/who.shtml
The Evangelical Fellowship for Lesbian and Gay Christians (EFLGC), formed in 1979, is a group of women and men, most of whom are lesbian, gay or bisexual and come from an evangelical Christian background.

http://www.mccchurch.org
Metropolitan Community Churches is now a worldwide network but was founded in 1968 in California as the world's first church group with a primary, positive ministry to gay, lesbian, bisexual, and transgender persons.

http://www.imaan.org.uk/
Imaan is a social support group for lesbian, gay, bisexual and transgender Muslims, their families, friends and supporters and those questioning their sexuality or gender identity.

http://www.safraproject.org/about.htm
The Safra Project is a resource project working on issues relating to lesbian, bisexual and/or transgender women who identify religiously and culturally as Muslim.

http://www.jglg.org.uk/
The Jewish Gay and Lesbian Group, JGLG, founded in 1972, is the longest established Jewish gay group in the world.

http://www.questgaycatholic.org.uk/home.asp
Quest, a group for lesbian and gay Catholics, is a registered UK charity and has a network of local groups across the country which meet regularly for Mass, discussion and social events.

http://umaffirm.org/
Affirmation: United Methodists for Lesbian, Gay, and Transgender Concerns is an active caucus of LGBT people and allies.

http://www.affirmation.org/
Affirmation Gay and Lesbian Mormons serves the needs of gay, lesbian, bisexual and transgender LDS and their supportive family and friends through social and educational activities.

Supporting teachers: legislation, guidelines and generating teaching ideas

Our work with teachers has demonstrated that primary teachers in the UK are not fully aware of the degree to which addressing sexualities equalities in the primary classroom is supported by legislation and policy. Failing to enforce LGBT equalities legislation provides a disservice even to children who make homophobic comments as they will eventually find themselves in workplaces where these kinds of comments are not tolerated (Purves, 2006). While it may be ironic to think that top-down mandates might be liberating, some teachers have argued that unless everyone is required to promote LGBT equalities as a school-wide response to national policy, individuals who promote LGBT equalities are seen as serving their own special interests (DePalma and Atkinson, 2006a).

On a national level there is recent positive legislation to support LGBT rights in the UK that will have implications for schools. The introduction of the Civil Partnership Act in December 2005 means that increasing numbers of same sex parents who have legal status as partners are still not recognised by their children's schools. Teachers and parents who have civil partnerships, and their children, rarely feel free to share their news at school in the way that news of weddings is often shared. The Civil Partnership Act supports teachers in representing same sex headed families in literature and discussion of families and relationships, since the rights of these families are now legally recognised.

Protection for transgendered people is provided in the form of the Gender Recognition Act (2004) which enables trans people to gain full legal recognition in their acquired gender, for example the right to marry in their new gender and to have their birth certificates altered to reflect their new gender.

In 2004, The Department of Health and DfES jointly supported the publication of *Stand up for us*, which aims to help schools challenge homophobia through developing a culture and ethos that promotes the emotional health and well-being of the whole school community. For each of the ten areas for whole-school action identified by the National Healthy School Standard (NHSS), criteria and guidelines are provided for assessing and improving the school's approach to homophobia. The 33 criteria include the following:

- homophobia is considered where possible across the curriculum

- the school actively engages with local LGB support services and others

- resources used in schools are inclusive

- the school's commitment to challenging homophobia and homophobic bullying, and to creating a safe learning environment for all pupils, including those who are LGB, is made explicit to all members of the school community

- there is support for LGB staff to be open about their sexuality

- pupils take responsibility for some aspects of work on addressing homophobia and homophobic bullying

- the school makes clear to all parents and carers that any information about their personal circumstances, including their sexuality, childcare arrangements etc would be welcome and will remain confidential.

These guidelines treat homophobic bullying as a cultural phenomenon and schools as a cultural institution whose change will require sustained, collective and proactive effort. In terms of classroom practice this cultural shift will require an inclusive curriculum paralleling the recent movements for inclusion of other marginalised groups. We recommend that the history, contributions and experiences of lesbian, gay, bisexual and transgendered people should be incorporated across the curriculum and not simply relegated to sex education. While it will be a great victory when homosexuality is included in discussions of sex and relationships, there is a danger of limiting sexual identity to nothing beyond sexual acts.

Even in contexts such as the UK where teachers may find considerable legislative support for including LGBT equalities in their inclusion agenda, the fact that this has rarely led to implementation means that teaching ideas and materials are still hard to come by. In February 2005, Schools OUT, an organisation working for LGBT equality, initiated the first annual LGBT History Month with financial support from the DfES. Guidance and teaching resources are available to teachers who want to celebrate the event in their schools (www.lgbthistorymonth.org.uk). Stonewall's three-year Education for All campaign, initiated in January 2005, also provides teaching resources and support materials on its website (http://www.stone wall.org.uk/education_for_all/).

Nevertheless, since most teaching resources so far available in the public domain are geared towards secondary schools, primary teachers are faced with the task of creating their own, or modifying existing resources which are intended for older children or that address other equalities. In the following section we describe a UK project based at the University of Sunderland in collaboration with the University of Exeter and the Institute of Education, University of

London, alongside a nationwide group of teacher-researchers who will design and evaluate their own LGBT-inclusive classroom and school projects.

No Outsiders: Researching approaches to sexualities equality in primary schools

Everyone is an insider, there are no outsiders – whatever their beliefs, whatever their colour, gender or sexuality. Archbishop Desmond Tutu (25 February 2004)

No Outsiders is a collaborative action research project that brings academics and practitioners together as co-researchers, enabling teachers to implement and evaluate strategies to address sexualities equality in their schools in a collaborative practitioner-research community. Funded by the Economic and Social Research Council (ESRC) and led by Principal Investigator Elizabeth Atkinson at the University of Sunderland, the project involves fifteen teachers in schools spread throughout the UK who are conducting action research projects in their own schools during each project year (2006-7 and 2007-8). The projects vary but all will explore strategies to address lesbian, gay, bisexual and transgender equality in primary schools.

No Outsiders belongs to the field of critical social research (Harvey, 1990), the purpose of which 'is essentially to contribute to educational transformation' (Crozier, 2003, p.82). Within the broad paradigm of action research we take a Participatory Action Research (PAR) perspective, which derives particular benefits from collaboration within and across research communities. The teachers will be supported throughout the project by three regional research assistants, each based at one of our collaborating universities: The University of Sunderland, The University of Exeter and the Institute of Education, University of London. Teacher-researchers will be collaborating in their own schools with research assistants in collecting, analysing and interpreting data. Linked by regional and national meetings, as well as an interactive project website, members of the research team form a global action research community (Somekh, 2005) which investigates its own practice with the goal of informing policy and practice.

At the first national meeting in September 2006 teachers and research assistants met for the first time to begin planning projects to be implemented between January and July 2007. In the meantime research assistants meet regularly with teachers for planning and to become familiar with the school and classroom environments. The results of the action research projects will be disseminated via a wide variety of media. Ideas and resources generated by teacher-researchers will be submitted to the online Teacher Training Resource Bank, funded by the Teacher Development Agency (TDA). An edited book of teaching ideas and resources and a specially commissioned documentary film are also planned.

This project was inspired by what was perceived as a lack of teaching ideas and materials that might help teachers address sexualities equalities in the primary school, alongside concerns about the lack of recognition of institutional homophobia and heterosexism in schools. For this reason we are keen to disseminate research results and emerging resources as widely as possible. We started this process even before the project began by compiling an annotated bibliography of LGBT-friendly books, ranging from picture books to young adult novels which are appropriate for readers in the upper primary age range. These books portray same sex parents, challenge gender stereotypes and feature gay and lesbian protagonists. Each teacher in the project is provided with a pack of books selected from this list. In the appendix to this book there is a snapshot of some of these books, as reviewed by members of the No Outsiders research team. For the full book list, which is a work in progress, or for further information on the project, visit the project website (http://www.nooutsiders.sunderland.ac.uk).

We hope that the No Outsiders project will contribute to initiating a culture shift in our project schools. Little by little, beginning in a few classrooms around the country, teachers are beginning to queer the norm so that institutional homophobia and heterosexism are no longer an automatic part of the primary school landscape. We hope that our small islands of change will eventually join up with other small islands of change and that these will inspire others, so that eventually school children will wonder whatever homophobia was about in the distant past.

Notes

1   We use the term 'sexualities equality', because we feel it evokes most clearly the concerns and issues being addressed. However, we acknowledge that there are champions of LGBT equality who would oppose this position, feeling that it is vital, above all, to be clear about the LGBT issues we are addressing.

2   These results were not published, but the investigation was undertaken to contribute to *Stand up for us*, see below.

3   This unpublished data was collected in and around the London area between May 2004 and May 2005 as part of Beatbullying awareness activities.

3

Confronting homophobic attitudes among traditional Muslim youth in Europe

Barry van Driel

Introduction

Homophobia in its various forms is still prevalent around the globe. Since there is no society where homosexuality is considered the norm, it challenges our imagination to envision what such a society would actually look like. For the moment, a key issue remains to what extent normatively heterosexual societies are willing to accept their homosexual peers as equals and to take steps to eliminate existing inequalities.

Many contributors to this book refer to societal contexts that are intolerant of homosexuality, especially conservative Christian communities in North America and Europe. Media reports and anecdotal evidence from educators on both continents point to one other community that rivals evangelical Christians in their disdain for gays and lesbians: traditional Islamic communities. This is not surprising given the common roots of Islam and Christianity and the many common values and themes in their two most important holy books: the Bible and the Qu'ran.

When attempting to confront the prevalence of anti-gay attitudes among Muslim youths in the west, some useful strategies will resemble those that tend to be effective with intolerant Christian youth. However, since each community and each individual is unique, when addressing homophobia in the Muslim community educators need to be aware of issues that will determine which strategies might succeed and which are more likely to fail. In this chapter, I outline the specific societal situation of Muslim communities in the west, how this influences identity issues and attitudes towards the Other and also which strategies are most likely to be effective.

Attitudes towards homosexuality in the Islamic world: still taboo and rejected but not a closed book

A cursory glance at predominantly Islamic societies across the globe today shows that members of the GLBT (gay, lesbian, bisexual and transgendered) community would face rejection, ostracism and in some cases much worse if they openly professed their sexual orientation[1]. Watchdog organisations like Amnesty International and Human Rights Watch have reported widely on the extreme punishments meted out to gays in for example the Middle East and the western media has picked up on these accounts.

The situation is dire in many countries. Six traditional Islamic countries still have the death penalty for same-sex intercourse: Saudi Arabia, Iran, Mauritania, Sudan, Somalia and Yemen, all located in the Middle East or East Africa. In many other nations, such as Pakistan, members of the GLBT community can expect imprisonment or other punishment.

The Pew Research Center's Global Attitude Survey in 2003 looked at the extent to which homosexuality was acceptable. The results show that a majority of people in all west European nations find homosexuality acceptable while this is definitely not the case in central and east European nations, the Middle East or Africa. Interestingly, people are more tolerant in some Islamic nations such as Turkey than in a Christian nation such as the Ukraine: 22 per cent versus 17 per cent acceptance – both relatively low.[2]

The issue of homosexuality continues to be more than a moral or religious issue in certain Muslim societies. In response to growing anti-Islamic sentiment in the west, exacerbated by the events of 9/11, the rejection of homosexuality has acquired added political dimensions. In the Middle East, as in Muslim communities across Europe, it is common to hear that: 'homosexuality does not exist in Muslim countries'[3], that it is an imported problem, anti-Islamic, or against the Arab nature. Politically, it has become a way to oppose Western influence and domination in the world and in the region[4]. Thus some influential conservatives attack gay rights, women's rights and human rights in general as an unwelcome imperialist agenda and import of the west.

According to Algerian human rights activist Anissa Hélie (2007), in previous centuries Arabs attributed homosexual behaviour to the bad influence of Persians. Ironically, at the turn of the nineteenth century, Europeans referred to same-sex relationships as the 'Persian disease,' the 'Turkish disease' or the 'Egyptian vice.' Conservative voices in Muslim communities currently attribute homosexuality to 'western deprivation'.

Although this might lead us to conclude that the situation in Islamic countries is hopeless, some countries such as Bosnia, Lebanon, Jordan and Turkey have been making efforts to ameliorate the situation.

In predominantly Muslim Bosnia, the new penal code in 1998 removed any reference to homosexuality – it has ceased to be a criminal offence. The law on Gender Equality, adopted in early 2003, now prohibits discrimination based on gender and sexual orientation. Cities like Beirut in Lebanon have a thriving gay subculture and a strong impressive gay rights organisation called Helem. Turkey has taken steps to legalise homosexuality and to protect members of the GLBT community from discrimination. These efforts are likely to continue as Turkey seeks membership of the European Union. However, homophobia remains widespread among the general population in these countries, especially outside the cosmopolitan areas. Many first generation immigrants from Muslim countries like Turkey arrived in the west with the attitudes that prevail in the communities from which they came.

Muslim minorities in the west: a history of distrust and survival

A recent history of migration

As the histories of the Ottoman Empire and the Moors in Spain show, European nations have always been multicultural and there has always been contact with Islamic cultures. However, the twentieth century can been characterised by what we might call 'the perfect storm'. The end of colonial domination and the independence of once subservient states and regions, combined with the emancipation and struggle for a new identity of their populace brought relatively large numbers of Muslim immigrants to countries such as France and the UK. At the same time, western Europe found itself in dire need of young and energetic workers for its newly booming economies. Such 'guest workers' and their families had a major impact on population demographics in countries like Germany, the Netherlands and Belgium. Finally, political and economic conditions around the globe led to another migration stream from the poorer and more unstable south to the richer and more stable north during the second half of the twentieth century. Most Muslim migrants who arrived in western Europe due to this migratory process trace their recent roots to poorer, more rural communities in already traditionally poorer countries.

Today, the total number of Muslims in Europe exceeds thirteen million and in some countries Islam has become the second largest religion. The figure of thirteen million represents approximately 3 per cent of the total European population (Buijs and Rath, 2002). This is still a relatively small percentage of the total population of Europe if compared to a traditional immigrant country like the United States, where the three big minorities – Blacks, Latinos and Asians – make up more than 30 per cent of the total population (there are some three to six million Muslims in the United States). Nevertheless, the growth of Islam in Europe has been swift. This growth is especially felt in urban centres and in urban schools. Due to *de facto* segregation processes, various school districts are now majority Muslim, but only in numbers, not in power or status.

Most teachers in Europe have not been trained to work with migrants from other nations, especially students with unfamiliar religious backgrounds, and especially around controversial issues such as homosexuality, or even general sex and health education (Sanjakar, 2005). Despite lofty ideals and stated concerns about this lack of training at international and national government levels, teachers rarely receive training, either pre-service or in-service, in how to address the needs of children from Muslim communities. Another cause of friction is that the large majority of Muslim students are taught by teachers from middle-class Christian backgrounds.

Though there has always been an uneasy relationship between Muslim youths and the majority population in Europe and a widespread sense among the youth of not fitting in, this relationship took a turn for the worse after the events of 9/11. The attacks fuelled the flames of already growing Islamophobia across Europe. More than ever before, Muslim youth, especially young men, now feel rejected, distrusted, unappreciated and marginalised. An increase in the general rejection by Muslim youths of western society, which is seen as immoral and decadent, has led to a corresponding increase in the rejection of the values that western schools attempt to transmit. Too often schools are viewed as alien institutions and anything but a haven in a heartless world.

It is important to understand this context if we are to design effective programmes for schools to tackle the homophobia among youth from Muslim communities.

Homophobia among Muslim youth: how serious is the problem?

The existence of high levels of homophobia among Muslim youth is the norm in Europe, but the situation is in flux and far from hopeless. Research in the Netherlands, which is the most permissive of all European societies towards homosexuality – Azerbaijan being the least – according to a 2005 European Values Study, illustrates this. In 1998, the organisation Forum (Institute for Multicultural Development) in the Netherlands commissioned research into the attitudes of Surinamese – who are mostly non-Muslim – Moroccan and Turkish youths towards GLBT issues. This took place in the context of alarming media reports of virulent homophobia among ethnic minority adolescents in the country.

The research, though small scale, showed that there were grounds for concern, but that attitudes were not as negative as portrayed. A key finding was that these youths had a large number of misconceptions and stereotypes about homosexuality. The general level of knowledge about homosexuality was minimal. Most youth also indicated that they had received little education about these issues either in or out of school, though they also indicated that they were open to such education. Almost all Moroccan and Turkish respondents indicated that they did talk with friends about sexual issues, but few talked to their parents about sexuality (85% and 71% respectively).

The majority of the young people interviewed were open to the possibility that their teachers might be gay or lesbian. But this did not imply a general acceptance of homosexuality, since there were low levels of acceptance of the possibility that a sibling might be gay or lesbian.[5] Some other interesting results were that Moroccan and Turkish youth were more open to the possibility that their female teachers were lesbian than that their male teachers might be gay.

A more recent study in the Netherlands points in the same direction (SCP, 2006). This general study into Dutch attitudes on homosexuality showed that there is still some general resistance in the Netherlands towards GLBT individuals – though less than in other countries. Some 22 per cent of the Dutch oppose homosexual marriage. It is striking, however, that among Dutch-Turks and Dutch-Moroccans these percentages are 55 per cent and 48 per cent. This implies that these immigrant communities are far less tolerant towards homosexual marriage than the majority. However, it also indicates that 45 per cent of Dutch-Turks and 52 per cent of Dutch-Moroccans do *not* oppose homosexual marriage. This is considerably higher than the support one would find in many other western nations.[6] These results suggest that Muslims in the west, though less tolerant towards homosexuality than their non-Muslim peers, have nevertheless become more tolerant of homosexuality than those in their country of origin. And this in turn suggests that attitudes in these communities are in flux and can be influenced in a positive direction.

Using the Qu'ran to challenge homophobia?

Can Islam itself and Islamic history be used as a tool to combat homophobia? Given the importance of the Qu'ran in the lives of traditional Muslims for their value orientation it is legitimate to ask whether it can be a tool in combating homophobia. This is the method some more progressive educators in the Muslim community are exploring. However, most intellectual discussions in this area focus less on how the Qu'ran promotes tolerance or understanding of homosexuality than on how this document condemns homosexuality. For example, scholar Muhsin Hendricks, a gay Muslim author and former imam in Johannesburg – before he came out – comments that:

> These modernist terms such as Homosexuality, Bisexuality and Heterosexuality by which modern society would like to classify humans are not terms found in the Qu'ran. There is however a theme of sexuality, sexual diversity and sexual perversity which runs through the Qu'ran and although the Qu'ran does address a larger heterosexual audience it does not imply that the Qu'ran condemns homosexuality. (*Huriyah*, 2006)

Elsewhere, this author talks about his organisation The Inner Circle and efforts to reconcile being both gay/lesbian and Muslim:

> Existing gay and lesbian organisations are largely secular. Hence they cannot fully support a person struggling to reconcile faith with sexuality. ... The Inner Circle is unique in the sense that it not only provides services to support queer Muslims, but also strategically fights homophobia in the Muslim community through education, training, research, and outreach. The model and strategy my organisation uses for social change is not geographically limited but can be implemented in Muslim contexts across the globe. (*Echoing Green*, 2006).

This perspective is also reflected in the words of Muslim-Canadian scholar Zahra Dhanani, who points to the story of Lot and Sodom and Gomorrah, which has been used by both Christianity and Judaism to denounce homosexuality: 'some scholars, like myself, interpret that as a condemnation of rape, not of homosexuals'. Though completely unacceptable in mainstream Islam, there are even gay Imams: Daayiee Abdullah is an openly gay Muslim Sheikh in the United States (*Metro Weekly*, 2006).

At present, such examples are rare within Islam. Though the Qu'ran can be interpreted in many ways, standard discussions of the issue of sexuality within Islam consistently point to the fact that sex is not a taboo in the Qu'ran. Neither are discussions of sexuality but, as is the case in the Bible, it is viewed exclusively within the framework of marriage or in the case of Islam within 'licit' relationships.[7]

It could be argued that, given the importance of the Qu'ran in Islamic communities, it should be a guiding light in education about sexuality and homosexuality, and that there are interpretations that would promote tolerance towards homosexuality. There are many pitfalls with using the Qu'ran, as there would be with using the Bible. For students who insist on interpreting the texts of the Qu'ran or the Bible literally for their moral compass, it will be more difficult to discuss homosexuality. It is easier to remove discussions of sexuality and homosexuality from this framework.[8]

Discussions about the history of Islam and Islamic societies can be a more fruitful approach than referring to the Qu'ran. It is not so difficult to point to the many Muslims of the past who were gay. For instance, Ibn Hazm (eleventh century), Ibn Daud, Al-Mu'tamid, Abu Nuwas and many others were writers who wrote extensively and openly of love between men.[9] More recently scholars have pointed out that Black American Muslim activist Malcolm X was bisexual.

Muslim associations devoted the GLBT issues
There are currently dozens of websites that cater to the needs of Muslim GLBT youth and the number is increasing. Most are located in Western countries since it is safer to conduct activities there but some have also appeared in Muslim nations. The existence of these websites helps GLBT youth feel less isolated. The sites are also an excellent source of information for students doing classroom projects on GLBT issues. Below is a brief list of some of the sites that cater specifically to those who identify as Muslim.

- A popular Middle East gay blog journal is: http://gaymiddle east.blogspot.com The site is political and is more for youth who are well-versed in the politics of gay identity. The many links to Middle Eastern GLBT organisations are especially interesting

- Organisation Q for Promotion and Protection of Culture, Identities and Human Rights of Queer Persons was founded in September 2002 in Bosnia and Herzegovina and formally registered in February 2004. Organisation Q is the first and only LGBT organisation in the country (http://www.queer.ba/udruzenjeq/en/udruzenje.htm) The site is in Bosnian and English

- Gay and Lesbian Arabic Society (GLAS), www.glas.org GLAS is an international organisation established in 1988 in the United States with local chapters in the United States, Lebanon and Egypt. It serves as a networking organisation for gays and lesbians of Arab descent or those living in Arab countries. The site is in English and Arabic. Another excellent US site is that maintained by Al Fatiha (http://www.al-fatiha.org)

- KAOS GL (www.kaosgl.com) is one of the main Turkish civil rights organisations devoted to combating homophobia. KAOS, created in 1994, organised the first International Anti – Homophobia Meeting in May 2006. This will now become an annual event. The site is in Turkish and English. Perhaps the largest GLBT organisation in Turkey is Lambda Istanbul (http://www.qrd.org/qrd/www/world/europe/turkey/), which defines itself as: 'a liberation group for gay, lesbian, bisexual, and transgendered people in Turkey'

- The Lebanese organisation Helem has chapters in six countries and is in English, Arabic and French (www.helem.net). Though focused primarily on Lebanon, the site contains extensive resources

- Aswat ('Voices'). According to its website, ASWAT is 'a courageous and dynamic group of women who have decided to organise to challenge the status quo and to improve their lives and hopefully secure these rights for the coming generations'.is the first openly-functioning organisation for Arab lesbians in the Middle East. Website: http:// www.aswatgroup.org/english/ Another site for lesbians is Bint el Nas (http://www.bintelnas.org/) It is in English and Arabic

41

■ Queer Jihad (www.queerjihad.com) defines itself as: 'the queer Muslim struggle for acceptance: first, the struggle to accept ourselves as being exactly the way Allah has created us to be; and secondly, the struggle for understanding among Muslims in general.' The website is in English

■ Huriyah (http://www.huriyahmag.com) This is a queer-identified magazine that contains excellent essays and articles about GLBT issues. The website is in English

■ LesMigraS (http://www.lesmigras.de/index.html) is a 'European-wide network of lesbian migrants, black lesbians, lesbian and migrants' projects and individuals, who combat multidimensional discrimination of lesbian migrants and black lesbians.' Though not exclusively devoted to Muslim lesbians, this is one of the target groups. The site is in English, German, Arabic, Turkish, Spanish and French.

Moving forward

These websites can all reduce homophobia among Muslim youth, but other strategies are also needed to find effective ways of moving forward.

It is important to look at the statistical reality. If there are some thirteen to fourteen million Muslims in Europe this means that more than one million must be GLBT, assuming that homosexuality is evenly distributed across cultures, religions, etc. This suggests that hundreds of thousands of Muslim youths are wrestling in some way with their homosexuality. It is a priority to support these GLBT youth by providing them with websites and phone numbers to use as resources and help them reconcile their religious beliefs with their sexual orientation.

For Muslim students who are not GLBT it is useful to distinguish between those youth who:

– are on the whole accepting of homosexuality

– are on the fence or undecided

– or who clearly reject homosexuality.

The aims of education may differ, depending on where somebody is located on this continuum. For students who are accepting, educators should aim to provide more arguments to support their tolerant opinions, to applaud their stance and to provide them with the skills to influence others, such as leadership training and better communication skills. Such students can become change agents in their community. With those that are undecided, the aim should be to move them closer to the more tolerant students and bring them into contact with each other. Those who reject homosexuality and homosexual rights often receive all the attention, for instance in the media, and their intolerant opinions can be resistant to change, especially if they have a religious or ideological basis. Many educational strategies target this group. In some ways this is unfortunate since interventions at this level can be counter-productive if not done professionally and sensitively. Interventions which target the other groups are likely to be more effective, because of peer group influences during the teenage years.

Certain conditions can promote the reduction of homophobic attitudes among those with more traditional Islamic beliefs. It is helpful to:

■ recognise the prejudice and discrimination that confront many Muslim youths today. If educators are willing to be empathetic towards their Muslim students and their experiences, chances are the students will also be willing to enter into an open dialogue about the 'pain' of others

■ embed the discussion in a human rights and antiracism framework. Many Muslim youths know what it is like to have their basic human rights violated and to be ostracised. This can be an excellent starting point for discussions about how different people cope with such ostracism, including members of the GLBT community

■ instead of trying to create sympathy for GLBT youth, use empathetic pedagogy, as Michele Kahn describes in her chapter

- In order to address controversial topics such as homophobia, prejudice and racism in the classroom, it is critical to create a space where students can express their opinions freely. This is a challenge for teachers who are unaccustomed to dealing with controversial issues or who do not know how to create a respectful climate of discussion in the classroom. There are a number of cooperative learning methodologies that can help, as well as out-of-school activities such as respect retreats (http://www.youthfrontiers.org/respect_retreat.html). Such retreats are becoming popular with middle and high school students in the United States

- respect the opinions of Muslim youths who express anti-GLBT sentiments, while challenging them without making them feel that they are being attacked personally and culturally or that their religion is being questioned or attacked. Otherwise, efforts can backfire and students can become oppositional or retreat from the discussion

- show that homosexuality has existed at all times and in all cultures. If possible have young people discover this through their own research, rather than lecturing them. The topic of homosexuality should not be exoticised

- invite openly gay Muslims to speak to the students as part of a larger lecture series on sexuality

- try to steer the conversation in the direction of solutions. Instead of asking students: 'why is homosexuality so problematic?' it is more effective to ask 'how can we all work together to reduce or eliminate homophobia, what first steps can we as individuals and as a class take or how can we make our GLBT peers feel more accepted and safe in our school?'

- For religious students who feel their belief system is threatened by talk of combating homophobia, remind them that they are not being asked to forfeit their religious beliefs but rather to take a stand against the harassment aimed at their classmates and peers.

While no one of the suggested strategies will alone eliminate the biases among many Muslim youths, in combination they should have an impact and improve the educational environment for all students. The support of GLBT Muslim youths, the professional training of teachers and the empowerment of already tolerant young people need to become a higher priority in the future.

Notes

1   *Guardian* newspaper journalist Brian Whitaker has recently written a revealing book: *Unspeakable Love: Gay and Lesbian Life in the Middle East* that details the secretive and often fearful lives of people in the Middle East seeking same sex partners. For more information, see: www.saqibooks.com The book was launched in Beirut in the English language but nevertheless was a bestseller for a considerable time at Virgin Megastore in Beirut. This demonstrates that the demand for such books is high.

2   Lebanon and Russia scored the same as Turkey (22 per cent acceptance). Countries such as Germany the Czech Republic scored above 80 per cent, while African nations like Kenya, Senegal and Mali and Asian countries like Indonesia scored at or below 5 per cent. In South Africa, 33 per cent were accepting. Canada scored 69 per cent and the USA 51 per cent. Full survey results can be found at: http://pew global.org/reports/pdf/185.pdf (page 114)

3   In March 1997 a university professor in Kuwait was fired because she had mentioned, in a private conversation with a student, her belief that there were lesbians in Kuwait. The female president of Kuwait University, who took the action to fire her, insisted, 'Ours is a Muslim society and homosexuality is against Islam' (AHBAB, 1996-1997).

4   Whitaker (2006) writes that: 'News media about same sex marriage and gay clergy in the West tend to be reported factually and straightforwardly by the Arab media, often with quotes from opposing sides.....The relatively calm tone of these reports in comparison with the more hysterical stories about local homosexuality ... They can be interpreted either as confirming Arab perceptions of Western decadence or as familiarising readers with alternative views of sexual behaviour. The problem, though, is that the dearth of coverage about Arab homosexuality encourages the idea that it is entirely a foreign phenomenon (p.72).

5   They were asked: 'Could you imagine that your brother/sister was homosexual? How would you respond to this? And how would your parents respond to this? (p. 91)

6   For instance, A Pew Poll in the United States in 2006 (Pew Research Center, 2006) showed that 51 per cent of people in the United States opposed gay marriage, making Dutch-Moroccans more tolerant than the average US citizen on this issue.

7   I would like to thank Khaled Diab for pointing this out (his website: http://www. diabolicdigest.net)

8   Though a risky course, one could argue that much of what is discussed in the Qu'ran is hardly relevant for today's world. For instance, the Qu'ran, written in the seventh century, is replete with references to slavery – a common practice at the time throughout the world.

9   **Abu Nuwas (8th – 9th century)**

Some claim that Abu Nuwas (full name: Abu Nuwas al-Hasan ibn Hani al-Hakami), 'Father of Curls,' named for his long flowing hair, was the greatest Arab poet of all time. This is one of his better known poems:

I die of love for him, perfect in every way,
Lost in the strains of wafting music.
My eyes are fixed upon his delightful body
And I do not wonder at his beauty.
His waist is a sapling, his face a moon,
And loveliness rolls off his rosy cheek
I die of love for you, but keep this secret:
The tie that binds us is an unbreakable rope.
How much time did your creation take, O angel?
So what! All I want is to sing your praises.

Love in Bloom

4

Dealing with diversity in education and counselling: lesbians and gays in German schools

Stefan Timmermanns

Far from widely accepted

There is no simple answer to the question about what it means to be openly gay or lesbian in a school in Germany today. The experiences are diverse and vary in different federal states, but German schools and educational institutions overall are unsympathetic to girls and boys who are in same sex relationships. Most teachers disregard the sometimes formidable problems experienced by gay and lesbian teenagers. The attitude towards gays and lesbians among the majority of young adults and teachers is still characterised by stereotypes and prejudices which are bred by ignorance and fear.

A representative study by the polling institute *iconkids & youth* in Munich has revealed that, at the beginning of the twenty-first century, 71 per cent of boys and 51 per cent of girls between 12 and 17 years of age reject lesbians and gays as 'not desirable' or 'not at all a good thing'. In my study (Timmermanns, 2003) I identified prejudices and stereotypical attitudes among a significant number of young people. Many believed that lesbians and gays could be recognised by their distinctively different appearance or gender-untypical behaviour: 'You recognise gays by their eye make-up. They speak like women and walk like women.' (Girl, 16). Some statements revealed revulsion and disgust, as well as the fear of being sexually molested or even raped by gays or lesbians: 'When I see a gay man, I am always afraid that he might rape me.' (Boy, 14).

Some typical examples from everyday life at German schools in the last few years will illustrate the many negative experiences that are part of lesbian and gay realities:

- A teacher at a Catholic girls' school was summarily dismissed from his post after he had formalised his life partnership with a man at a magistrate's court

- A female teacher verbally abused not only her pupil when he outed himself in his class, but also his mother when she attempted to have a discussion about it.

In its six-part series SOS School, the German television station ZDF reported on 3 May 2006 that a pupil at a Berlin comprehensive school was harassed by his fellow pupils because he had told them of his infatuation with another boy at his school. From that moment, nobody wanted to sit next to him. He became the target of abuse and hate speech and was attacked verbally and physically. Neither the teachers in charge nor a social worker specially appointed to assist in this difficult class could address the fears and prejudices of the youngsters or deal with the social isolation of the gay pupil. In the end, the pupil had no alternative but to leave the school. The only advice his teacher gave him was that to protect himself from more enmity and abuse in his new school, he should not 'advertise his affections'.

In 2000 the Ministry for Women, Youth, Family and Health in North Rhine-Westphalia published the *SchLAue Kiste* (Clever Box), sex education resource materials and methodological guidelines pertaining to same sex relationships and lifestyles. This led to vigorous debates in letters columns of various local newspapers, in which especially Christian groups accused the red-green coalition government of 'brainwashing' youth. Five years later the newly elected

Christian-Democrat-Liberal government in the same province suspended the distribution of the handbook *Different in More Ways Than One: Providing Guidance for Teenagers on Their Way to Identity, Sexuality and Respect,* a publication mainly financed by and developed within the European Union. A spokesperson for the Minister of Education justified these actions by stating that children and youth should not gain the impression that turning gay or lesbian would now become obligatory at school.

Although more young people now come out at school, difference in terms of sexual orientation is still inadequately addressed within educational institutions. The main reason for this is the lack of appropriate teacher training, not only on sexuality in general is concerned, but especially about homosexuality. The root cause can be attributed to an irrational anxiety on the part of teachers which leads them to avoid the topic: there is fear that talking about homosexual relationships will motivate youngsters to become gay or lesbian. It is more likely that the silence surrounding sexual orientation in its different forms will inhibit the personal development of gay and lesbian teenagers because there is such prejudice against homosexual lifestyles in schools and in society generally, in spite of the fact that these have been decriminalised and same sex partnerships have now been legalised.

In Western industrialised countries the significantly higher suicide rates among lesbian and gay young people bear witness to this. Even though it has long been scientifically discredited, the old theory of youths being 'seduced into homosexuality' still haunts German pedagogy and educational philosophy. Most people believe that same sex love is an unacceptable subject to discuss with children and young people. Young lesbians and gays are left to their own devices during their coming out. With the exception of a few organisations in large cities there is no personal or institutional help or support for young people during this critical phase of their lives.

The guidelines for sex education have been revised in most federal states in recent years so that it is now possible to deal with same sex relationships in a way that does not tie the discussion to the darker sides of sexuality such as prostitution, paedophilia or 'perversions'.

Especially in Germany's northern states sex education aims to contribute to reducing discrimination against gays and lesbians and to promote tolerance and respect. However, this curricular change alone cannot lead to more open communication around gay and lesbian issues: a serious commitment to respecting diversity and abolishing discrimination against minorities must include the appropriate education and training of staff.

Tried and tested ways of working against homophobia

For more than 20 years lesbians and gays, most of them young, have been active in German schools and have shared their life stories to encourage other young people to walk their own paths with confidence. There are about 30 such voluntary projects in Germany, to make school classes and youth groups more aware of same sex lifestyles in an enlightened educational practice. In 1999 and 2000, I mentored and evaluated some of these projects in North Rhine-Westphalia and described the results in *Keine Angst, die beissen nicht!* (Don't worry, they don't bite!) (2003). The study showed that participants had significantly higher levels of tolerance and acceptance after their engagement with lesbians and gays. Their way of viewing homosexuals became less stereotypical.

In some of the educational projects two men or two women led the class. Consequently many young people formed a more differentiated picture of gays and lesbians: 'One of them was very gay, was dressed like a gay. The other looked like a normal heterosexual.' (Pupil,16) More than half the teachers reported that after the pupils had completed the module on homosexuality the atmosphere in class was much less sexist and homophobic. Long-term effects could not be established due to the time schedule of the study. However, it can be assumed that the success of a single intervention can only be sustained when there is support from the school community and when dealing with this subject is not an isolated event left for outsiders to deal with.

It is crucial to the success of such educational projects that the teachers are qualified. Most of the active volunteers in the project are students or people in formal employment and many of them are studying in the educational field. With a number of educational projects now networking under the umbrella of SchLAu NRW (Schwul-Lesbische Aufklärung in Nordrhein-Westfalen/Gay and Lesbian Awareness programmes in North Rhine-Westphalia) and with the creation of a similar structure on a national level, the quality of lesbian and gay awareness programmes should soon improve – especially with the increase in in-service training options in Germany alongside communication and discussion of common goals and methods.

Unless practitioners in mainstream pedagogy become competent and knowledgeable in this area, the efforts of young gay and lesbian volunteers in the field can have only limited impact. In addition to qualitative and substantive improvements in training and continuing education programmes, there is an urgent need for the development of teaching and learning materials on same sex lifestyles for a wide range of pedagogical activities.

The textbook *Different in More Ways Than One* (2004) is a first step in this direction. It was the result of a transnational project, financed by the EU, under the auspices of the Ministry of Health, Social Affairs, Women and Family in the federal state of North-Rhine Westphalia. The handbook includes background information, didactic guidelines and short stories. It is a valuable tool for schools, youth centres and counselling clinics to deal more competently with sexual orientation and with ethnicity and to work against the discrimination against young lesbians and gays. The book was developed and tested by experts from five European countries before it was released on the internet in German, English, French, Italian and Dutch (www. diversity-in-europe.org). It is particularly suitable for working with adolescents and young adults. It would be good if local authorities all over Germany would actively promote the distribution of this educational resource in schools.

Martin Ganguly in Berlin has published a special life orientation booklet to promote the integration of same sex lifestyles for children and young people. It appeared at the Humanistischer Verband Deutschlands (Humanist Association of Germany) under the title *Ganz normal anders – lesbsch, schwul, bi* (Quite normally different – lesbian, gay, bi) and is an excellent resource for teaching across the curriculum in primary schools and also in more senior years. It is structured according to age and offers teaching modules on topics like role specific behaviour, living together, preventing violence and discrimination, getting to know each other, and being different. All the elements can be used individually or in varying combinations. Many creative methods are explored, such as painting, arts and craft, dressing up, role playing, story telling and changing the narrative perspectives of fairy tales and stories.

What can teachers do?
Building on the school curriculum
In a large institution there needs to be a solid base to work against discrimination. There may be a paragraph in the mission statement of the school where respectful interpersonal communication is set as a goal and discrimination is rejected in principle. It should be explicitly stated that nobody should be exposed to discrimination on the basis of gender, ethnic origin, disability, age, sexual orientation or sexual identity. This statement should be developed through an inclusive process with all concerned, especially the students. In this way teachers will be empowered to speak about sexual orientation in class, and to take action against discrimination. The notion that parents do not approve of these measures is usually a feeble excuse offered by those who themselves find this topic difficult. The contrary is true. On the whole parents are reassured to know that their child is protected against discriminatory practices at school. It is important to be aware of all possible reasons for discrimination. Where rigid structures make such an inclusive approach difficult or impossible, individual initiatives are to be encouraged, if necessary without the sanction of school management or of the entire institution.

What is the situation of my target group?
What are the previous experiences of the young people in my class when it comes to issues of homosexuality? What do they already know about same sex lifestyles? To what extent have they had concrete experiences with lesbians and gays? What is their cultural and religious background?

The answers to these questions will determine both the appropriate themes and the methodology. Where learners have little experience or where cultural or religious influences have created strongly negative attitudes, the teacher should work in a low profile way and strive to avoid confrontations and provocations. It is advisable to work first from the basis of the learners' experiences and existing knowledge and only then facilitate other cognitive and emotional approaches to the subject.

To determine the students' existing knowledge a simple questionnaire will suffice, or an exercise in completing sentences, such as: 'Lesbians are ...... They engage in ...... They should/may ......' Learners can complete similar sentences about gays and heterosexual men and women. The exercise can end with the sentence 'I have learned all of this from ....'.

The comments are then collected and in the discussion that follows it is important to interrogate sources and stereotypes critically and to stress the amount of diversity in each group. This exercise has a two-fold aim: to encourage opinions to be voiced and to share feelings. Moreover, the teacher gains an overview of the range of emotions, values, attitudes and questions regarding sexual orientation and identity and general issues of sexuality within the group.

How can we cope with negative and disruptive behaviour?
How can homophobia be addressed in the face of probable strong rejection? One reason for prejudice may be a strongly religious upbringing. Another may be students' inability to cope with their own negative emotions that cannot be integrated, balanced or mitigated through positive experiences or rational arguments. Negative judgments about homosexuality must be taken seriously and their root causes explored. Mostly they arise from fear or ignorance. Everyone has his or her personal feelings and attitudes towards homosexuality and bisexuality. To deal with this situation successfully, young people should be given the space and the time to explore their feelings and articulate their experiences, fears and concerns.

Rather than prohibit discriminatory remarks at the outset, these should be recognised for the potential discussion topics they contain. They can be the starting point in the common search to find ways of developing new and respectful communication. It is possible to overcome resistance among learners through an inclusive and holistic approach which creates an atmosphere of trust and acceptance. Only then will they be open to arguments and prepared for self-reflection. They should have the opportunity to voice prejudices and stereotypes without fear of censure. When dealing with cultural diversity teachers and counsellors should find out where and how their students are living so that they feel acknowledged and accepted. Limits can be set from the outset, mindful of the existing knowledge and the attitudes of the young people: discriminatory remarks and gestures should no longer be tolerated after an agreed point.

What should I remember in my planning?

The next task is to formulate realistic goals for the groups and identify suitable methods for achieving them. Depending on the situation at the start these goals may have to be modest: tolerance instead of acceptance. Students should not be expected to approve of homosexuality but they should also not disparage people who have openly gay, bisexual or lesbian lives and should not insult them or try to reform them. Mutual respect is essential. Someone who personally rejects homosexuality should be able to say so openly and respectfully without fear of being ridiculed or verbally attacked.

Nobody has the right to feel that their person or lifestyle is inherently superior. If young people feel provoked by lesbians or gays this should be brought into the open. The cause of this behaviour is often rooted in heterosexual norms and not necessarily in a desire to be provocative. Even if a homosexual person were to make a pass, heterosexual persons can learn to turn this down in a relaxed way without feeling threatened in their own sexual identity and orientation. Young people reject heterosexual advances regularly without this causing conflicts.

Extend background knowledge and give information

The first step is to expand the concept of sexuality beyond the sexual act itself to include thoughts, dreams and fantasies. It is equally essential to understand that there are differing sexual orientations and that human sexual behaviour and sexual feelings are better understood as located on a continuum rather than in rigid categories. This can be illustrated by the scales developed by American sexologist Alfred Kinsey, who based his research not on how people described themselves but on their actual sexual activities. Knowing that a certain number of people live their sexuality in certain ways can relieve anxiety and also the fear that all people might have homosexual experiences some time in their lives.

Although a relatively small proportion of the population, lesbians and gays are a numerically significant group whose rights must be respected and who must be protected against discrimination. However, the way a minority is treated should not depend on their statistical significance. This leads to the arena of universal human rights, international documents, and the country's Constitution or Bill of Rights, especially where these refer to the individual's right to free development of their personality. A comparison with other discriminatory practices related to ethnic origin or disability, and a discussion of laws which prohibit such discrimination would also be relevant.

Create new ways of gaining access – emotions as key

When planning a discussion about homosexuality it is a good idea to start with a gay and lesbian awareness project. This enlivens discussion and adds authenticity to the process but may not always be possible because voluntary groups cannot offer comprehensive programmes in every community. Where this resource is not available books or films are a viable alternative and role play is also useful.

Marco Kreuzpaintner's film 'Sommersturm' is recommended to introduce the topic of a gay coming out in Germany. A teacher's manual for the film is available from the *Bundeszentrale fuer politische Bildung* (www.bpb.de/publikationen/P8FRCP.0.0.Sommer sturm.html). The materials and methods all aim to create empathy and a degree of identification for as many young people as possible, especially to understand what it means to be different from the majority and to be forced to conceal an integral part of your personality for long periods of time to avoid being stigmatised and treated like a social outcast.

The role of the teacher when dealing with values and norms

In an intercultural context, establishing a common set of values without allowing any single group to dominate is an enormous challenge. It is important to identify commonalities as well as differences but above all not to neglect the unifying elements between cultures. A crucial norm that should be established is that there is mutual respect. Discrimination of any kind in the group should be prohibited. To avoid confrontational lines being drawn between the opinions of students and an attitude of political correctness being imposed from above, the teacher should strive to remain in the background. Their function is to provide support when one faction threatens to dominate and others are intimidated into silence about their opinions. The teacher should not attempt to proselytise in any way as this would be seen as interference in students' private sphere and interpreted as undue influence. A teacher's role is to facilitate between different opinions in the class and when necessary to remind the class of the principles of democracy. Teachers have the right to state their personal opinion but this should not influence the ultimate evaluation of the students.

Since emotions are always evoked in discussions about sexual orientation, norms and values, they should be addressed in class discussions or in small group work. This should be an opportunity to articulate and explore emotions without denial or value judgements. Provided that they are expressed in an acceptable way, negative emotions should not be suppressed or stigmatised by the teacher. Sometimes the aim can be to learn to articulate rejection in a way that does not offend others. When students express revulsion or abhorrence, they should be exposed to other experiences in order to learn from them. Discussions become more concrete and credible when pupils or even the teacher talk about the personal experiences with lesbians and gays, and the learning process required when, for example, a (perceived) sexual pass is understood to have been made by a person of the same sex.

Providing help and support for someone coming out successfully is another task for teachers. By adopting the bridging and counselling functions embedded in several German curricula on sex education, teachers can guide (young) lesbians, bisexuals and gays towards facilities, organisations and programmes which offer support locally or through the internet. Other issues also need to be pursued, such as striving to create a social environment that accepts and approves same sex orientation.

Teachers need to be empowered to run these sessions. Unfortunately, there is a dearth of training programmes in Germany that deal with sexual orientation, life styles, discrimination and human rights. The aim of such programmes should be to strengthen the capacity of the individual to reflect and extend the knowledge of the discipline as well as teaching competence. Self-reflective processes help teachers become aware of their own motivation when teaching and give priority to the students' needs rather than their own goals.

Multiplicity as a concept

When dealing with sexuality the focus should initially be on the variety and individuality of what it means to be human. People of different ages, nationalities, gender, character can be introduced so that young people are offered different role models and there is less opportunity for stereotyping. Giving a positive emphasis to variety also means that commonalities are sought and identified. The principle of variety contains contradictions because people are both different and similar: commonalities and differences exist concurrently and on the same plane. We have to learn to live with the resulting tensions.

The methodological concept and didactic approach contain similar characteristics: it clearly makes sense to include anti-discrimination concerns or incorporate sexual orientation when designing lesson plans. Themes around life orientation, gender and sexuality can be addressed in literature classes or in foreign language teaching by reading biographies or novels for young adults. Moritz Gleitzman's award winning story for children and young adults *Two Weeks with the Queen* (1998) can be read in English class and Chris Donner's novel *Lettres de mon petit frere* (1991) would be suitable in French classes.

A good choice for cross-curricular history and German teaching would be Lutz van Dijk's novel of the persecution of homosexuals during the Nazi era, as illustrated in the story of a relationship between a Polish youth and a German soldier: *Damned Strong Love* (1995). But even apparently neutral subjects like mathematics and science can be made sensitive to issues of difference by formulating problems in such a way that human variety is reflected. Civics and citizenship education, the social sciences, political science and history are rich terrains of discovery about how sexuality was handled in other cultures and epochs. Through paintings, sculpture and music, opera and musicals, etc. the arts offer a wealth of information about human relationships, love and sexuality. The main aim should be for young people to engage with themes in a personal way to interrogate norms and values critically and to find their own attitudes and positions.

What methods should I use?

Working in small groups, possibly segregated by gender, makes for an intimate conversational space and can be a positive experience: a greater variety of opinions can be heard than in the larger group. Reporting back in a plenary session can facilitate a summary of the work done and an opportunity to identify commonalities and differences. Those who are more reticent can write their questions or opinions anonymously on slips of paper or index cards and place them in a closed box. It is important to have rules for discussions and to adhere to them consistently. In this way a trusting and supportive atmosphere can be established. A few basic rules give learners more confidence and promote respectful communication within the group. These rules may include:

- everyone has the right to finish what he or she wants to say

- everyone speaks for himself or herself, and

- there is nothing that cannot be said – but nothing has to be said.

Methodology which focuses on emotions ranks alongside story telling as a powerful tool, especially where real life stories are told. These can take place in a roundtable discussion with lesbians and gays or through the medium of literature. The stories of young lesbians, gays and bisexuals contained in the handbook *Different in*

58

More Ways Than One work well. The book contains a wealth of background information and many hints for dealing with issues around sexuality, life styles and multiculturalism at school and in youth groups. The stories depict everyday reality and especially emotions which connect closely with the real life experiences of young people such as being in love, experiencing heartbreak, stress and tension within a relationship, conflicts with parents and refusing to be defined by social role expectations. Young people can identify with these situations and realise that fundamental human experiences such as love, sorrow, disappointment, joy, enthusiasm, and affection are a common bond for all people, irrespective of their gender, origin, religion or sexual orientation.

This chapter is translated from the German by Karin Chubb.

Translator's note: The literal translation in the official English version of the German Constitution (page 55) is 'the right to self-fulfillment'; I think that is vaguer than 'the right to the free development of the personality' also commonly used, and have therefore chosen the latter.

Part 2
Beyond Schools: from support groups to constitutional rights to university settings

5

Educating about sexual and affective diversity in Spain: the challenge of turning legal equality into actual equality

Jesús Generelo

To understand LGBT issues in Spain we need some understanding of the conflictual history that Spain went through over last 30 years. This will also afford insight into the present situation of the Spanish educational system.

Now that Spain has overcome a period of cultural isolation imposed by Franco's forty year dictatorship, it has achieved considerable advances experienced years ago in other countries. During Franco's rule, Spain was officially a Catholic country and national Catholicism, with its conservative sexual rhetoric, enabled church hierarchy and doctrine to strongly influence the law, public policies, norms, education and even many details of everyday life (Roca, 2003). Recently, however, Spain has developed a nation with high standards of liberty. This has helped this country lead the way in the struggle for recognition of the rights of sexual minorities.

This rapid transformation has brought about legal equality between heterosexuals and homosexuals. Spain is one of the few countries where same gender couples can get married. However, are these achievements the result of an historical pendulum that has made Spanish society reject extremes? Or is this a real success story, deeply felt by everybody and anchored in people's minds?

The majority of the Spanish population has a favourable attitude towards homosexuality and homosexual individuals. According to the *CIS* (Spanish Sociological Research Centre), 66 per cent of Spaniards were in favour of homosexual marriage in 2004. Images of homosexuality and transsexuality abound in the mass media, literature, in the streets and in the lives of many Spanish citizens. But there is little mention of any of this in Spanish education. Pupils who watch television, listen to the radio, hang out in community spaces and surf the internet will encounter openly gay or lesbian people, families headed by homosexual parents, or relatives and friends who are known to be homosexual or transsexual. But once they enter their classrooms this subject disappears and there is an assumption that all pupils are straight. This situation casts some doubt on the future of present day liberties. This is why COGAM (*Colectivo de Lesbianas, Gays, Transexuales y Bisexuales de Madrid*) is convinced that direct educational measures are needed that will reinforce these advances, especially around attitudes towards sexual diversity.

One aspect of Spanish education needs special mention. The Autonomous Regions into which the country is divided make decisions about educational policies. The Spanish government provides the guidelines for the educational system, but the Autonomous Regions manage, interpret and develop them. The conservatism of some of these regional governments, particularly those ruled by conservative parties, make it problematic in a political, structural or legal sense to incorporate discussions about sexual diversity. Because of this COGAM's education department has always been on the cutting edge of activities in this field.

Twenty per cent of schools in Spain are private and Catholic, although the government provides them with financial aid to cover the *ESO* [Obligatory Secondary School] costs. Catholic religion must be offered as an option in all schools, whether public or private. The syllabus for this subject was developed not by the Ministry of Education but by the *Conferencia Episcopal* (Spanish Organisation of

Catholic Bishops). Consequently, the influence of the Catholic Church is strongly felt whenever public institutions attempt to modify any detail of the values they try to transmit.

COGAM is therefore committed to talking about sexual diversity in its educational work. This chapter describes educational policies which, if they were to be exposed, would most certainly meet with resistance. The strategies do not offer a permanent solution but they help to open some doors in a besieged system and to help the educational community to incorporate a reality that was troublesome until now.

Education laws in Spain

In 1990 the government of Felipe Gonzalez tried to revolutionise the education system by putting into place the LOGSE act (Spanish General Act for Ruling the Education System). The purpose of this act was to change the way various subjects are taught in Spain. The new approach focused not only on knowledge but on the transmission of a set of values. Groups of teachers were to become educational teams engaged in more complex pedagogical projects. The values of a new democratic society, such as peaceful conflict resolution, health, eradicating discrimination and respecting sexual diversity, were to be thoroughly analysed in all subject areas.

These good intentions failed because they were not supported by resources, such as providing the means for training and selecting teaching staff. The task of transmitting values was taken up by a few good-hearted teachers. One of these values was respect for sexual diversity. Very few teachers felt compelled to take this on so only the luckiest pupils received sex education, which was usually limited to a quick explanation of the reproductive system and sometimes information about using condoms as a way to prevent pregnancy.

In early 2006 a new act replacing the *LOGSE* act was passed, called *LOE* (*Ley Orgánica de Educación*). One of its explicit principles is 'the recognition of sexual and affective diversity'. It proposes a new subject: Education for Citizenship and Human Rights. The subject encompasses topics such as rejecting homophobia and recognising different types of families, including those involving homosexual parents. The subject is only taught in secondary school and in the last two years of primary school, which implies that these topics are still linked to the willingness and insight of teachers in the earlier grades. The syllabus is under attack by conservative forces. As this book was going to press, Catholic conservative groups successfully lobbied to remove the terms homophobia and family diversity from the subject curriculum. Also, Madrid's public schools, presently under right-wing Party rule, will not be implementing ECHR until 2008, the deadline for all communities in Spain to add this new subject to the preparation taking place in their teaching centres.

Action Guidelines of COGAM's Education Department

COGAM's education team is made up exclusively of volunteers. When the Education Department of COGAM was established in 1996, in a worse socio-political environment, we started only with good will and the knowledge that any progress would be difficult. Nevertheless, 'education within values', proposed by the LOGSE act, was used to convince the education community of the need to develop programmes around sexual diversity issues. Despite the obstacles to access Spanish educational structures, there are always loopholes and allies to work with. So, for the past ten years, we have been planning the following activities, always complemented by the necessary political lobbying efforts:

- action programmes for schools
- teacher training
- developing educational materials
- encouraging research.

Action programmes for schools

The main COGAM programme consists of *in situ* activities developed by our volunteers for schools that request this service. It was inspired by the one implemented by The Dutch Association for Integration of Homosexuality ('COC') in the Netherlands in the early 70s, and has been quite successful so far. Every year, we offer schools in the Autonomous Region of Madrid the opportunity to participate in this project. Two volunteers, a gay and a lesbian, spend one hour in each class. The school decides on which groups participate.

For fifteen minutes these volunteers explain a series of concepts which might be unknown to pupils: the definition of sexual orientation, gender identity, how to identify homophobia, how homosexuality is discovered and accepted, what coming out of the closet implies for a young person and the global situation of sexual minorities. This sparks a discussion in which all comments are allowed so that pupils can reach their own conclusions. We do not indoctrinate pupils – although we have been criticised for doing so – but engage them in open discussion. Occasionally we do role plays so that pupils can get more involved in the discussion and relate to issues that have been raised.

We are aware that this programme is inconvenient for some and various groups collaborating with COGAM in other Spanish regions have decided not to support it. They offer the following reasons for their reluctance:

- Interventions by a volunteer association allow the education system to escape its responsibility in addressing these issues. If teachers allow COGAM to take the lead, they can ignore their own civic duties

- Since this programme is not managed by the *Consejería de Educación* [Education Department of Madrid], volunteers will never reach all schools because they are free to request or refuse our services

- The concept of transversal action does not apply when working with sexual and affective diversity. We agree that homosexuality and trans-sexuality are not subjects that should be treated separately, outside the realm of general sex education. Sexual orientation and gender identity are part of sexuality, so we must not send the message that certain subjects are unique and that they need to be studied separately. Its detractors think that by implementing our programme we somehow encourage self-exclusion.

Despite these criticisms, COGAM continues to emphasise sexual diversity for a number of reasons:

- Even though teaching staff have to work within diversity and they need to show pupils the social reality around them, many teachers do not feel attracted to the subject matter. For straight pupils, meeting people who openly state that they are LGBT makes them empathise with them in a personal way. To increase empathy, we try to link volunteers and pupils who are approximately the same age. Several studies have shown that meeting homosexuals decreases people's homophobia[1]

■ For pupils from sexual minorities or those with an uncertain orientation, having points of reference is essential. Meeting a gay or a lesbian in person who might not fit the most well-known stereotypes portrayed in the media, and whom one can identify with, can be significant

■ Having a LGBT association within the educational sector can reduce apprehension among staff about discussing homosexuality in an educational context. The COGAM programme has succeeded in that teachers who have participated pass on the concept when they move to another school, explain the programme to their colleagues, and remove fears of conflicts with parent associations or with education authorities. Eventually the annual visit paid by our volunteers normalises the debate on sexual diversity and compels educators to face their responsibility in this field.

Our evaluation of the COGAM programme has been extremely positive. From the questionnaires pupils of several schools filled out we conclude that they consider our sessions to be interesting, informative and entertaining. Some pupils even described them as an impressive personal experience. According to the teachers' reactions we can also deduce that they find the programme interesting, since the schools that participate keep requesting our services and we receive more requests every year. After the national debates about homosexual marriage and the passing of the new law allowing these unions, the demand for our programme has increased sharply.

Teacher training

In Spain attention has not yet been focused on how teachers should be trained. Nowadays, at the ESO, teachers are required to have a university degree and a short pedagogical training which is not an effective preparation for their appointment. It means that higher priority is given to subject knowledge than pedagogical skills. It is a challenge to ask teachers to focus more on the educational process than on educational content. Training teachers to teach effectively about sexual diversity is an even greater challenge.

Our strategy has been to develop training courses for teachers together with different institutions, like *Centros de Apoyo al Profesorado* [Madrid Network of Support Centres for Teachers]. We have had some success but have had to be tactful, giving courses ambiguous names since references to homosexuality might elicit resistance. Only in this way have we been able to gain the approval of school principals.

Our collaboration with teacher unions has been more effective. The *Consejería de Educación* and the Ministry of Education finance training courses developed and organised by the unions. As a result we have developed several courses in association with the *Comisiones Obreras* Union. In addition to knowledge transference, these courses focus on the personal transformation of teachers. This is done by implementing methods and activities which promote values such as respect for gender identity and sexual diversity, using an empathetic but critical approach. Methods used include role play, expressive body movement, discussion forums, exchanging experiences and life stories. The underlying theme of these courses is that the professional training of a teacher is based not only on the acquisition of information and processes, but also on attitudes. Above all, we are battling with the remnants of internal homophobia. We attempt to address not only ignorance but also the emotional correlates of homophobia. Our last workshop was entitled 'Transforming myself to transform' because we believe that the transformation of teaching staff has a multiplicative effect for children, for young people and through them for the whole of our society.

We have to acknowledge that our activities only touch on the problem of teaching staff having limited training, or lack of skills or resources to satisfy the demands of a pupil population that lives in a plural society in terms of sexuality. At present our aims and the size of our target group need to be modest. Those who attend our courses are teachers who care most about the topic and in some ways we are preaching to the converted. Early evaluations show that our participants are primarily women (lesbian or straight) and gay men. Few straight men are willing to have their heterosexual worldview challenged for the benefit of their pupils.

We are carrying out pioneering activities that are slowly removing some taboos that seemed impermeable. The importance of these courses is not in the number of teachers who have been trained but in the fact that our programme helps to define future educational debates. We are starting to have an impact at the policy level. For instance, we are struggling to include subjects in the new syllabi of education departments that relate to the sexual diversity of pupils and their families, as well as to homophobia in classrooms. In this way future teachers of *Educación Infantil, Educación Primaria* and ESO can study these topics in the public universities of Madrid.

Developing educational materials

The lack of materials in the Spanish language that address sexual diversity is one of the most widely mentioned issues by teachers who want to address the topic. In 1998 the Children's Ombudsman, associated with the regional Government of Madrid, published an educational booklet entitled *25 cuestiones sobre la orientación sexual* (25 questions about sexual orientation). This guide, written by our education team, was distributed three times in every Madrid high school, and several times in different regions (see www.cogam. org).

The object of this booklet was simple: to present a handbook on the subject, divided into a series of basic questions with clear and simple answers. If we had assumed that teachers would know the answers to these questions, we were wrong. Our experience showed that they held many misconceptions. Our experiment was deemed so risky that the Children's Ombudsman decided to exclude any reference to homosexual families from the guide. The Children's Ombudsman and COGAM were accused of sexually harassing children, though the guide was made for teachers. The contents were modified in such a way that some media said that the text 'encouraged children not to talk with their parents'!

During 2005-2006 we wrote two new guides in association with *Comisiones Obreras* union: one for teachers ('*Diferentes formas de amar*') [Different ways of loving] and another one for pupils ('*El amor y el sexo no son de un solo color*') [Love and sex do not have only one colour]. The former goes beyond the original 25 questions; it offers various resources and goes deeper into the topics. In some ways these materials are more adult, showing that Spanish society has gone beyond a rather childish attitude towards sex. The latter, still in press, is addressed to all students regardless of their sexual orientation or gender identity. In this booklet against homophobia, we confront stereotypes and we urge educators to respect differences and to struggle against sexism and homophobia.[2]

What these guides have achieved, apart from the significance of being published, is collaboration with institutions that have given their 'stamp of approval'. It opens many doors. For educators, the fact that a guide has been certified by the Children's Ombudsman and the *Comisiones Obreras* Union gives them self confidence. First, they can be sure that the product is of high quality, meaning that it is not merely a biased pamphlet written by a gay group. Educators that elect to use the materials can feel supported in case they are criticised for their choices.

We are also developing a book for *Educación Infantil*, consisting of nine educational units, which can be used with children from 3 to 6 years of age, which will include a guide for teachers. The book is being coordinated by COGAM members and teachers from public schools are participating in the project. We understand that we need to work on eliminating homophobic attitudes and behaviour from an early age.

Encouraging research: the importance of data

In Spain little scientific literature or fieldwork has been conducted on homophobia and the school situation of LGBT adolescents. Such data is critical to make an even stronger case for sexual diversity education in the future.

COGAM's Education Department has signed an agreement with the Department of Social Anthropology at the *Universidad Autónoma de Madrid* [UAM] since we wanted to know exactly the extent of homophobia in the education system. BA students in Social Anthropology turn to COGAM every year so that they can prepare a research paper. In 2004 they were asked to develop a qualitative study that focused on the perception of homosexuality in classrooms and the harassment suffered by LGBT adolescents in schools. This work, linked to related research on the same topic by members of our education team, led to a piece of research entitled *Homofobia en el Sistema Educativo* (Homophobia in the Education system).

This study revealed what we had claimed for ten years: homophobia is still prevalent in a large number of pupils. There is a high degree of ignorance about homosexual and transsexual life among adolescents and sexism and homophobia are common phenomena, so that LGBT adolescents live in a risky and inequitable educational environment.

These findings showing real data, plus as the reputation of the UAM, attracted the attention of the mass media. Spanish left-wing parties, such as *Izquierda Unida* (IU) and *Partido Socialista Obrero Español* (PSOE), took this study on board to launch proposals in several regional parliaments that would combat homophobia in schools. In the end the Spanish parliament approved a proposal put forward by the PSOE, asking the government to implement a specific plan against sexism and homophobia in schools.

The strategy of considering homophobia to be a product of sexism has proved to be useful in the Spanish context. In this approach homophobia is seen as a consequence of a rejection of the feminine in society, associated with traditional conceptualisations of masculinity. The approach has worked because some well-intentioned politicians have always found good reasons to link sexism and homophobia. Although these individuals might find it difficult to include the words homosexuality or homophobia in their speeches, references to the traditional sexist system makes the arguments legitimate for voters.

At present, our Department is finishing the anthropological study *Adolescencia y Minorías Sexuales* [Adolescence and Sexual Minorities], in association with the UAM to identify the different realities and troubles experienced by LGBT adolescents.

Jumping to conclusions: does our present situation represent a final chance?

In this chapter we outlined strategies that have been put into practice within a context of cultural conservatism and religion. Our standard working procedure consists of dodging obstacles, profiting from existing loopholes and seeking minor agreements at the beginning that become more important towards the end. We are determined to trust that increased visibility is our best leverage. Our experience tells us that most manifestations of homophobia are not due to radical ideological rejection, but to ignorance.

Clearly, our present-day educational system differs completely from that of only ten years ago. Education is still under siege but Spanish society has a clear opportunity to move forward in the area of education for citizenship and human rights. It is legally possible to show Spanish children that homosexual families exist and that homophobia is harmful. The government will need to become more involved in eliminating the risks that LGBT pupils experience every day. This may be the right moment to tackle this problem in a structural way, something that was impossible until recently. We are convinced that we need to engage pupils in the early education phases. What pupils learn early on will influence their attitudes and behaviour in later years.

This chapter was written in collaboration with the COGAM's education team, composed of Belén Molinuevo, Octavio Moreno, Ignacio Pichardo and Mercedes Sánchez Sáinz, and translated from the Spanish by Jorge Toral.

Notes

1   See '*Investigación sobre las diversas actitudes hacia la población adolescente escolarizada de la Comunidad de Madrid* [Research on the different attitudes to adolescent people enrolled in schools in the Autonomous Region of Madrid] (1996-97) and 'Homofobia en el Sistema Educativo' [Homophobia in the Education system] (2005), both written by COGAM's Education Department, in addition to further studies conducted in other countries. Various documents can be found at: <http://www.cogam.org>

2   This booklet includes the fabulous comic Le Monde de William translated into Spanish, created by the ExAequo Association in Belgium.

6

Confronting homophobia in UK schools: taking a back seat to multicultural and antiracist education

Debbie Epstein, Roger Hewitt, Diana Leonard,
Melanie Mauthner and Chris Watkins

Teacher: And this is how it was explained to me by the deputy head of [another school] and I actually stand by it. With racism most kids know the boundaries, it's political, they know the boundaries, you ring up the parents there is some form of support. In this school there would be lots of support from certain areas

RH: Yeah

Teacher: You'll get a response, sexism you'll get a response but maybe not as much as the racism. Homophobic, in that particular school, and I think it's the same in this school, is most of the parents are just as homophobic they won't admit it openly but they are just as homophobic and it gets said in the house and it's the norm.

(Appletown. Interview with Roger Hewitt[1])

Introduction

People make themselves but not (to misquote Marx 1963) in conditions of their own choosing. In doing so both identifications (Hall, 1996) – who you identify with, want to be like and want to be with – and dis-identifications (Skeggs, 1997) are important – who you dislike, hate and are repulsed by. In school contexts identifications and dis-identifications are frequently made along lines of social difference and are enacted through practices of exclusion, derision and bullying. The conditions for identity production are in part produced by public school policies. Here, we focus on one particular area of dis-identification: homophobia highlighting how this contrasts with how antiracist work is contextualised.

Now you see it ...

Many authors have discussed the extent of homophobia within schools (Mac an Ghaill, 2000; Nayak and Kehily, 1997, and Letts and Sears, 1999) in Anglophone countries. They have addressed the experiences of lesbian, gay and bisexual students, explored how heterosexual masculinity is constructed through qualitative work or contributed to our knowledge of the prevalence of homophobia in schools through quantitative surveys (Douglas *et al*, 1997; GALOP, 1998; Rivers, 1995).

Our research in UK schools has also shown that homophobia and heterosexism were visible to staff and students alike. The use of homophobic language and the incidence of homophobic abuse were frequently mentioned and many commented on the regular use of homophobic terms such as 'pooftah' and 'batty boy' and on the punishments meted out to anyone but especially boys who appeared to be 'gay'. Anything from smiling at someone, to touching someone accidentally, or saying a stupid thing could result in being called gay, which is considered a horrible insult.

Research has shown the persistent race and racism in schools since Bernard Coard's (1971) key intervention in his pamphlet *How the West Indian child is made educationally subnormal in the British school system*. The changing ways in which racism operates have been amply demonstrated (Gillborn, 1990; Troyna and Hatcher, 1992; Blair, 2001; Gaine, 2005 as well as the journals *Race, Ethnicity and*

76

Education and *Race Equality Teaching*). Work about race and racism is increasingly focused on strategies for addressing and combating it (Epstein, 1993; Dadzie, 2000; Knowles and Ridley, 2006) and it is clear from the literature that teachers in schools are aware of the need to adopt these strategies (Ali, 2003). As Mirza (2006) points out, the story of tackling racism and its effects is far from successful, with good intentions being drowned out by the press of bureaucratic paper work.

But at least racism is firmly on school agendas, particularly since the murder of Stephen Lawrence in 1993 and the report which followed (Macpherson, 1999). Both caught the headlines for some time in the UK. This is in contrast to questions of heterosexism and homophobia which have only reached school agendas and public policy and then only patchily in the past few years. Current work by Elizabeth Atkinson and her colleagues (reported in the *Observer* 11 March 2007 and followed up in other news media the following week) is starting where multicultural/antiracist education was in the mid-1980s. Just as it is easy for journalists to find Christian and other religious spokespeople to protest about Atkinson's work now, it was easy for them to provoke protests about antiracist work in the 1980s (Epstein 1993).

Now you don't ...

When asked about sexist, racist and homophobic abuse, many teachers responded that homophobia was a particular problem in their schools. Others ignored this aspect of the question completely, as if it had not been asked. Thus teachers from the same school gave different views. For example, at City Heights, one teacher commented that, 'there are homophobic, terrible homophobic attitudes' Whereas another teacher said:

> In my four years here I've yet to receive, erm, when you say 'homophobic'. I mean kids are going to call each other gay as a cuss, but it's, erm, I've not dealt with a case where I've dealt with a gay student yet, so I can't really speak for that. I have not dealt with that situation yet, so it's not a problem for me or anything like that, but I've just not dealt with one yet. So, but, erm, kids always, you know, cuss each other, that kind of think, you know, mother cussing is always rife. (Information provided in interview with Melanie Mauthner)

The underlying assumption of this teacher is that if she is not aware of lesbian, gay or bisexual pupils in the school, homophobia is not a problem. The homophobic incidents reported by both teachers and students were almost invariably to do with name-calling, verbal harassment and bullying and rarely involved physical violence. This may explain teachers' tendency either to ignore or not take these events seriously (see Carrington and Short, 1993; Epstein and Sealey, 1990 and Gaine, 1987, 1996 on similar findings in relation to race in white schools).

Much contemporary work on masculinities and schooling links homophobia to the construction of male identities (Epstein, 1998; Gilbert and Gilbert, 1998 and Nayak and Kehily, 1997) while anti-lesbianism has its own gendered dynamic. Part of the route taken by many boys towards establishing themselves within school hier-archies takes the form of macho laddishness. This performative masculinity is a powerful way for boys to establish themselves as definitely heterosexual and they use homophobia and misogyny as resources for the construction of their masculinities (Willis, 1977; Martino, 1999, 2000).

Struggling with policies

The schools we researched all had clear policies and practices to respond to racism. While these may not always have been success-ful, school management teams felt that they knew what they were doing and there was apparent consensus amongst staff and most students that racism was not acceptable or defensible.

Parental and local cultures of homophobia are a problem for schools trying to combat homophobic bullying and harassment: this was raised by a number of teachers in the schools. There was a strong feeling that there would be problems in making homophobia an issue for effective policy and practice. Teachers who considered it an important issue were quick to point out potential difficulties and why homophobia lagged behind racism and sexism in being dealt with.

Teacher: With homophobia it's quite difficult because you've got kids here that are fundamentalist Christians, kids who are Methodists, kids who are born again Christians and those kids don't respond. As far as they are concerned it's against God, so therefore... And it's trying to educate them to accept that they may have these religious views, however, they are not acceptable within the school framework. And that's quite hard. I think that is difficult and I think it's hard for all school really, because of the age that the kids are and the fact that it's not as clear cut as the black and white thing. It's you know 'It says in the bible'.

RH: Do you think it's therefore in conflict with some sort of multi-cultural ideas?

Teacher: I think so. I think it is if I am perfectly honest. Because I think it's very very easy for a group of kids to unite because some one is picked on because they are black. I think the majority of kids I teach now, I hope, would be able to unite on the same basis on the fact that some person is being picked on because of their sexuality, but I know that there will be two or three in that group that would either overtly, or inside, be thinking 'Yes, but they are a homosexual. Why should they be given the same rights' and I think it's an ongoing issue. They reflect society. It's an ongoing debate in our society, and that's why in that sense we cannot fit an ivory tower in here. Their parents say these things. (Daleford teacher, interviewed by Roger Hewitt)

This teacher, from Daleford School, attributed the difficulty in dealing with homophobia to the presence of religious fundamentalists within the school. His head teacher's explanation was more along class lines:

Head: No, I'm just trying to think. Racist is, racist is most comprehensively [addressed] I suppose in terms of equal opportunity policies. And in fact we're quite successful with that. Not that many, I can't think of that many exclusions that have a racist sort of basis. And kids, I think, are pretty much aware that you don't say those things. It's only very rarely it happens with particular kids possibly or a very odd situation. So while kids fight they, by and large, don't appear to fight from a racist cause. Sexist is more, the kids are more likely to say sexist [things], the company of sort of 'slags' and that sort of thing comes and they don't have the same taboo and would use that. But whether that actually leads to violence, I can't think, I would never really of looked sufficiently to see if it does.

I think it does quite often, I mean there are fights and arguments between boys and girls but I'm not sort of ... And homophobic, I don't think we've addressed that, it's much more difficult to address and it doesn't come up so obviously amongst kids in school. Particularly in working-class areas I suspect. And so we often talk about the fact that we should do more about ... But it's the racist one probably that the school has worked at hardest and is possibly the one that would have been most combustible if we hadn't.
(Interview with Roger Hewitt)

These teachers all explained that policies to deal with homophobia lag a long way behind those to combat racism and sexism though they were struggling to take up this issue. Various teachers completely ignored the issue of homophobia while being seemingly sensitive to other forms of prejudice and discrimination.

Strategies for the future: changing policies, changing practice

Ofsted (the official UK inspection agency for school) is quite clear on issues of homophobia in the UK. It has recommended that:

Schools should make sure that values relevant to education about sex and relationships are consistently adhered to within the school so that, for example, homophobic attitudes do not go unchallenged. (Ofsted, 2002: 34)

It is clear that schools have a responsibility to develop better policies and practices to challenge homophobia, not just to protect those young people who identify as lesbian, gay or bisexual but in the interests of reducing the levels of violent incidents that take place at and around school. The question is what initiatives schools should take.

The first step is for all teaching and other staff to inform themselves of the issues involved in homophobia and heterosexism. This can take place within the context of staff development and the development of policies owned by all staff. But involvement of the staff alone is not enough: as with other policies it is important that parents, governors and students are also part of the picture. The issues will not go away if they are ignored and people will not be convinced just by being told they are wrong.

Some may anticipate a possible clash between multiculturalism/ antiracism and anti-homophobic practice. Clearly, these are difficult issues but it is not enough to stop at that recognition. Neither is it tenable to say that one demand for social justice outweighs another. Consequently teachers need the skills and understanding to be able to deal with this complexity and this needs to be clear to everyone associated with schools. The first rule has to be that neither homophobia nor racism are acceptable in schools and both will have certain consequences. Teachers can take comfort in the fact that parents are usually far more accepting of policies than they fear. This was the case in the early days of antiracism and continues to be the case with anti-homophobic/heterosexist work. What is key to parents is that their children are taught in a positive and respectful school environment. Democratic and open exchange of views is important here but it is a mistake to think that democracy is the same as consensus. Democracy relies on principled respect for the other and sometimes on agreement to disagree (Epstein, 1993).

The thorny question, 'how do we deal with conservative Muslim/ Christian parents/children' needs to be addressed. The key strategy is simple: children should be well-taught and happy in school. This is the main concern of most parents. If such basic needs are taken care of dissatisfaction with schooling does not become displaced on to anti-homophobic policies. The key issue is that schools need to be clear that they do have these policies, that they are a statutory requirement in the UK and will be adhered to. One of the main findings in the project from which this chapter derives is that the schools that were most successful in reducing violence and bullying of all kinds were those that were consistent in their approach and whose policies were owned, known and carried through by all staff. Objections to this work can be met through addressing parental concerns about violence and bullying. Neither parents nor children are happy about bullying and are usually responsive to strategies to reduce it.

Schools which work with both perpetrators and victims – who are often the same people – and their parents to understand what is going on and why are often the most successful in reducing it. The fact that homophobic bullying is directed at many children, especially boys, who do not identify as gay, lesbian or bisexual offers a way in here.

It is futile to try to address these issues directly through appeals to religious texts and histories when one does not adhere to the faith in question oneself. This is likely to produce defensive reactions. But there are religious groups, such as the Lesbian and Gay Christian Movement, respected figures such as Archbishop Desmond Tutu, and organisations such as the Safra project for Muslim lesbian women, which may be called upon for support. These are listed on the No Outsiders website (http://www.nooutsiders.sunderland.ac.uk/about-the-project/religious-support-for-lgbt-people). There are schools, including those with high numbers of Muslim and other religious pupils, who have developed good practice in this area and other schools can look to them for a lead. These examples, found by the No Outsiders project, will be placed on the Education Department's website in due course. Just as teaching about and against racism must start from where the students are, so does teaching about and against homophobia. It is no use becoming didactic and authoritarian since these strategies are likely to produce a homophobic school counter-culture. Equally it is negligent to ignore homophobia because of the difficulties that dealing with it might provoke.

A pedagogic process needs to take place, not just in relation to students but with other stakeholders in the school as well. It is important for coherent and consistent approaches to be developed, and that whole school policies are in place and are put into practice in reliable and predictable ways so that staff, students, governors and parents all know that they can be counted on.

A note on resources
We are fortunate that there are now several excellent and easily obtainable resources for developing work to reduce and prevent homophobia in the UK.

- The Department of Education and Skills (http://www.dfes. gov.uk) has numerous links to pages that offer evidence and advice about homophobia. This can be found by going to the DfES website and doing a search for 'homophobia' or by going directly to http://www.dfes.gov.uk/search/results/kb search?qt=homophobia&sc=dfes&ha=1

- *Stand up for us* (Jennett, 2004), developed as part of the National Healthy Schools Standards, offers numerous practical and thoughtful approaches to combating homo- phobia in schools and can be found at http://www.wired forhealth.gov.uk/PDF/stand_up_for_us_04.pdf

- The No Outsiders research project has an excellent website with links to a comprehensive range of resources. It can be found at: http://www.nooutsiders.sunderland.ac.uk/

This chapter is drawn from Epstein *et al* (2003) and the work of *The 'Violence-Resilient' School: A Comparative Study of Schools and their Environments* project, funded by the Economic and Social Research Council (Award No L133251041) as part of its *Violence Research Programme*.

7

The only country on the continent: realising constitutional rights in South African schools

Dawn Betteridge and Lutz van Dijk

'Based on dignity, equality and freedom...' – the new Constitution of South Africa

In 1996 South Africa's constitution became the first in the world to prohibit unfair discrimination on the grounds of sexual orientation. It thereby guaranteed equality for gay and lesbian people[1]. Just as this section of the constitution specifically mentions race and ethnicity in response to South Africa's past of discrimination and racism, sexual orientation is included due to the injustices gay and lesbian people have suffered in the past. Since December 2006, same sex marriage became part of the legal family code, making South Africa one of the few nations in the world that accept same sex marriage.

Moving away from the intolerant past

Before the new constitution was ratified, sexual activity between two people of the same gender was considered a crime and public displays of affection were considered to be indecent. Gay people were frequently harassed and blackmailed by the police, often denied employment and refused custody of their children after divorce.

Gays were both persecuted and prosecuted, while lesbians were largely ignored. Men were arrested for lewd and inappropriate behaviour and seemed to be particularly targeted through conservative legislation against pornographic materials. Any advocacy groups that were in existence operated underground.

One of South Africa's most bizarre and notorious anti-gay laws was introduced after a police raid on a gay party in a suburb of Johannesburg in 1966. Amendments to the Immorality Act resulted in the infamous 'three men at a party clause', which criminalised any 'male person who commits with another male person at a party any act which is calculated to stimulate sexual passion or give sexual gratification'. A 'party' was defined as 'any occasion where more than two persons are present'.

....towards a more promising future

The relevant part of section 9 of the new South African Constitution, entitled *Equality*, states that:

> The state may not unfairly discriminate directly or indirectly against anyone on one or more grounds, including race, gender, sex, pregnancy, marital status, ethnic or social origin, colour, sexual orientation, age, disability, religion, conscience, belief, culture, language and birth.

In 1996 the Constitutional Court unanimously declared that both the previous common law crime of male 'homosexual sodomy' and several statutes incorporating that crime for various purposes violate the new constitution. The court held that all convictions of 'consensual sodomy' dating back to the adoption of the interim constitution 1993 were subject to invalidation, which was a landmark ruling, not only for South Africa but for the continent of Africa.

The interim constitution of 1993 and the permanent new South African Constitution from 1996 both provide in a Bill of Rights that 'everyone is equal before the law' and prohibit 'unfair' discrimination on the basis of sex and sexual orientation, as well as a large list of other characteristics. The constitution also explicitly protects the right to privacy, and states that rights enumerated in the Bill of Rights may only be limited in a manner that is 'reasonable and justifiable in an open democratic society based on human dignity, equality and freedom.'

Many factors played a role in ensuring these provisions. One was a commitment from the former liberation movement and present ruling party, African National Congress (ANC), as well as individual members of the ANC, to ensure rights for all, in recognition of the role that lesbians and gays had played in the Anti-Apartheid movement. Another was the continual commitment of LGBT groups to lobby for their rights.

As High Court Judge Laurie Ackermann[2] explained:

> Just as apartheid legislation rendered the lives of couples of different racial groups perpetually at risk, the sodomy offence builds insecurity and vulnerability into the daily lives of gay men. There can be no doubt that the existence of a law which punishes a form of sexual expression for gay men degrades and devalues gay men in our broader society.

His colleague, Judge Albie Sachs, emphasised the importance of managing differences in a democratic society:

> The invalidation of anti-sodomy laws will mark an important moment in the maturing of an open democracy based on dignity, freedom and equality. As I have said, our future as a nation depends in large measure on how we manage difference. In the past difference has been experienced as a curse, today it can be seen as a source of interactive vitality. The constitution acknowledges the variability of human beings (genetic and socio-cultural), affirms the right to be different, and celebrates the diversity of the nation.

> The fact that the state may not impose orthodoxies of belief systems on the whole of society has two consequences. The first is that gays and lesbians cannot be forced to conform to heterosexual norms. They can now break out of their invisibility and live as full and free citizens of South Africa. The second is that those persons who for reasons of religious or other belief disagree with or condemn homosexual conduct are free to hold and articulate such beliefs. While the constitution protects the right of people to hold such beliefs, it does not allow the state to turn these beliefs, even in moderate or gentle versions, into dogma imposed on the whole of society.

Constitutional rights and everyday reality – still a huge gap

More than a decade after the new South African Constitution was ratified opinion polls in South Africa clearly indicate that overwhelming majorities of citizens are still 'against gays and lesbians' and that homosexuals are doing something 'wrong, disgusting, un-ethical, un-African', to quote just some of the remarks. Such remarks have also been expressed by some political parties who especially 'treasure family values' (like the African Christian Democratic Party, ACDP). In open hate speech, for example in letters to newspapers, sexual minorities are also referred to as 'perverts and AIDS carriers.' In conservative rural areas or poor townships they are called 'tomboys' and their behaviour is declared by African traditionalists as 'un-African'. Most Christian churches and most Muslim faith groups are unified in condemning homosexuals as 'sinners' and 'truly against God and Allah'. It is often the same group of 'law abiding citizens' who also advocate the re-introduction of the death penalty which was abolished in the new South African constitution.

Research conducted by centres against violence, human rights groups or LGBT organisations show that women and men who claim their constitutional rights as homosexuals and who become visible in their neighbourhood, family or school are still taking a serious risk of being harassed and even physically attacked. A most recent survey in KwaZulu-Natal, one of the South African provinces with the highest HIV-infection rate, has shown that out of 292 black lesbian women who were interviewed, nine of them had been raped, fifteen had been subjected to physical abuse and 40 to hate speech for being lesbian. In KwaZulu-Natal the average HIV-infection rate among pregnant women (the only group with reliable figures) is between 25-30 per cent, whereas the average infection rate in South Africa is estimated at 10 per cent of the population.

From time to time the murder of a young woman or man makes sad headlines. One of the latest was the brutal killing of 19 year-old Zoliswa Nkonyana[3], which was widely reported in the press. Zoliswa was attacked by a mob in February 2006 in front of her home in Khayelitsha, the largest township outside Cape Town. Her partner, a 17 year-old girl who preferred not to be named, told the police that they were just walking home when another schoolgirl confronted them by calling them 'tomboys who wanted to be raped'. Within a short time this schoolgirl was joined by about twenty young men who felt challenged to follow up on the vicious insult. According to her partner, Zoliswa told the schoolgirl: 'We are not tomboys, we are lesbians. We are just doing our thing, so leave us alone'. She described what happened next as follows:

> They beat Zoliswa in the face. I said to her we must run but she said: 'No, this is my area, why must we go?' Then they started beating both of us with a golf club... When I was on the ground I managed to get up and run away and climb over a fence. Zoliswa was also running towards her home but they caught up with her. They were again beating her, some throwing bricks and one stabbed her with a knife. She was just lying down but they kept on.

Zoliswa's stepfather finally ran out of their home and only realised when he came closer that the victim was Zoliswa. She was bleeding and couldn't speak anymore. He managed to bring her to the local hospital where Zoliswa died shortly after admission. Her mother, who was praying in church while the killing happened, said later:

> When I saw my daughter there I was so sad and so afraid... I knew Zoliswa was a lesbian from when she was eleven. I went to the shop to buy her clothes, but the child didn't want a skirt. She liked to wear boy clothes... She told me later she liked girls.

Together with other lesbian girls from her area in Khayelitsha township, Zoliswa had started their own soccer team, called the Winnie's Soccer Club. They regularly trained and felt safer together. All members of her club came to attend her funeral and helped to organise another 400 people who showed their compassion and sympathy for Zoliswa. In the neighbouring township of Gugulethu, a march of solidarity was held by about 150 lesbian and gay activists.

After a photo of Zoliswa with three of her friends from the soccer club was published in a local newspaper there were more threats. Zoliswa's girlfriend, fearing for her life, left the township and was moved to a safe place under the police witness protection scheme. Just over two weeks later six suspects were arrested, all males between 17 and 19 years of age. They were released on bail shortly after and a court date was set for six months later. To date no convictions have been made.

Jessica Stern, a researcher associated with Human Rights Watch in New York, observed:

Ten years ago, South Africa enacted the world's first constitution to protect against discrimination based on sexual orientation. Today it's both
tragic and telling that Zoliswa still could not be safe in her own neighbourhood.

The story of Zoliswa shows why confronting homophobia in the
classroom is so crucial[4]. It is here – in one's immediate daily environment – that young people develop their understanding, their language, their identity and ability to deal with diversity, positively... or
negatively. In Zoliswa's case, the spark that set off the murder was
another schoolgirl who obviously felt challenged in her own identity
as a heterosexual girl. She felt provoked by the mere existence of
Zoliswa and her friends, and their non-conformism as far as gender
roles are concerned. There was no conceptualisation that diversity
could be something positive, just one of 'eliminating' differences
through aggression and violence, in this case even a brutal murder.

Understanding sexual diversity in South African classrooms

A number of LGBT and human rights organisations in South Africa
train students and teachers about issues of equal rights, including
sexual orientation, which includes sexual diversity. However, none
are fully supported by the National Department of Education and
none form part of the national curriculum. There is some regional
and provincial support for individual programmes, but this does not
extend to financial support.

The way in which crimes committed against LGBT people are dealt
with varies tremendously from one police station to the next. The
Triangle Project in Cape Town has received reports about people in
township areas being turned away when trying to report crimes, being laughed at and told that they deserve it. In some instances people
have reported being abused by police officers. However, there have
also been reports of crimes being treated in a sensitive manner so it
is not possible to generalise. Clearly, there is no generally agreed approach within the police force, but sensitivity is the exception rather
than the rule. Hate crimes against LGBT people are not registered in
any special way, as they are in other countries, which makes it difficult to analyse crimes against LGBT people statistically.

The Triangle Project

The Triangle Project was named after the pink triangle gay men had to wear in German concentration camps during Nazi times. It is one of the oldest gay liberation organisations in South Africa and they celebrated their 25th anniversary in 2006. The organisation started during the apartheid era as GASA 6010 (Gay Association of South Africa, Cape Town branch) as a predominantly white and middle class organisation. They changed their name in the late 1980s to ASET (AIDS Support and Education Trust) to focus on HIV/AIDS prevention and counselling which in those days was still regarded as a gay disease. In 1996 they reopened under the name Triangle Project. Their head office is in Mowbray, Cape Town, with different outreach programmes in seven townships. They operate mainly in the Western Cape province but cooperate and meet regularly with other LGBT organisations in other provinces. Their mission is 'the development of a non-discriminatory society where organisations such as Triangle Project are a choice and not a necessity.' They believe in 'the dignity of lesbian, gay, bisexual and transgender people, our right to live and contribute meaningfully in society, our right to equal rights rather than special rights and development programmes as key to prevention of HIV/AIDS and other sexual transmitted diseases (STD) in the South African context.'

Education within the LGBT community and for society in general is one of the new approaches within the Triangle Project. Its aim is to achieve dignity for LGBT people. In 2005 an Educators Awareness Project named Understanding Sexual Diversity in the Classroom was developed with independent funding. It consists of three elements: a workshop manual, a two-day seminar and a power point presentation. The target groups are teachers in public schools, as well as educators in fields of child and youth care, police and health.

Eight steps are suggested in the manual pertaining to how this could be achieved[5]:

1. Why the need to address sexual diversity?

How do I see my role as a sexuality educator? Where have we come from? How to tune in to diversity language?

The South African Schools Act of 1996 calls for a new national system for schools: To redress past injustices, to provide an education of high quality for all learners, to advance the democratic transformation of society and to combat racism, sexism and all other forms of unfair discrimination and intolerance...

Mahatma Gandhi once said: '*We must become the change we wish to see in the world.*'... Do the words matter? For example, how does the power of words shape how we understand sexuality and sexual orientation? Find your way of expressing these terms... and compare your thoughts with our short definitions: Sexuality – the way we identify and express ourselves as sexual beings. Sexual orientation – whether we are heterosexual, bisexual or homosexual.

2. Exploring and knowing ourselves

Who am I? Are educators 'ideological virgins'? How can I become more sensitive to diversity?

As educators, we need to work through our own way of thinking on issues before we are in a position to influence and encourage learners and others who wish to explore the same issues...

Oscar Wilde once said: '*Learning to love yourself is the beginning of a lifelong romance.*'... To become more aware about issues like sexual diversity, we need to be open about what our ideas and feelings are. And to begin the difficult process of shifting and changing our attitudes. We may have to be humble, for example, about things we previously said or thought. We may have hurt someone by the language we used – for example, by referring to a 'real man' or by excluding a learner with a lesbian mother from a family day.

3. Developing ways to involve our learners

What methods will I use to reach the learners? What methods can I try to get things going? How can we use role-plays to learn about diversity?

We introduce some of the key principles and tools of participatory methodology: It encourages groups to be involved in identifying their own problems, discussing solutions and planning and then taking action...

A Chinese proverb says: '*Tell me, I will forget. Show me, I may remember. But involve me, and I will understand.*' Some of the key principles are: Self-esteem, creativity, action planning, responsibility and group-building... The example of role-plays: This is where you ask people to play certain roles and act a scenario – for example a learner asking parents for information about sexuality. You make clear that participants are playing roles that are not necessarily the same as who they are in real life – for example a girl who tells her mom in the role-play that she has feelings for another girl at school... List first some sensitive topics for yourself to do with sexual diversity in your class.'

4. Sexual diversity – questions and answers

What do I need to know about sexual diversity? How can education assist the learners?

Write down a few of the typical questions related to sexual diversity that your learners have asked you in the past, or that you expect they may ask you...

A young person once answered why she/he became homosexual with another question: '*So, when did you first discover that you were hetero-sexual?*' Eighteen often asked questions about sexual diversity are listed and provided with guided options of answers. Some examples: At what age do people know they are gay, lesbian or bisexual? Can you tell if someone is gay, lesbian or bisexual? Is sexual orientation a choice? Can therapy change sexual orientation? Is homosexuality 'un-African'? What does gay and lesbian sex involve? Let us give one example of a question and answer: In a lesbian or gay relationship, is one person always active and the other passive? Answer: No, the idea of a dominant 'male' role versus a passive 'female' role is an outdated concept that doesn't apply to most relationships anymore, whether straight or gay.

5. Sexual identity and development – childhood

Did I (when I was a child) understand these different – biological and gender – identities? How was my gender identity formed? Can we be agents of change?

Educators who are non-sexist and who do not stereotype boys and girls have an enormous role to play in promoting gender sensitivity. This approach can create space for children to express difference, and thus lay the foundation for education around sexual diversity.

A three year old boy said once while he was playing with dolls: '*I am not a moffie!*' [South African slang for 'faggot']. ... During childhood (ages 1 to 9), the infant's body image begins to form. Children continue to display genital curio-sity, and often physically compare themselves to those around them. ... Realise that healthy sexuality development begins at birth... Do not pre-empt a child's sexual orientation due to his/her gender and physical appearance... Treat girls and boys equally. Do not make distinctions between what boys and girls are allowed to do or to say... Consciously include examples of different kinds of relationships and families... Intervene when children engage in aggressive acts with sexual content.

6. Sexual identity and development – adolescence

What has been my own sexual identity formation? How do I gain access to stories of sexual identity development?

Sex and sexuality is important to all young people, whatever their sexual orientation. As they explore and discover their bodies and their sexuality, they need to feel empowered and that they will be not judged for having sexual feelings. This is even more important for the adolescent who experiences same sex feelings of attraction, as it is usually seen in a negative light.

The tennis champion Martina Navratilova said once: '*I was used to people mistaking me for a boy... big ears, big feet. 'I'm always going to look like a boy', I cried. 'Don't worry...', my father told me. 'I can tell you're going to be pretty when you grow up.'* ... The curriculum, lesson plans and class discussions cover mainly issues related to heterosexual children and youth. This means that young people who are struggling with their sexual identity often remain invisible throughout school... Fictional stories of two teenage girls (Brenda and Latiefa) and two boys (Vuyani and Paul) are given and analysed by the learners due to their physical identity, gender identity and sexual orientation.

7. Sexual identity and development – adulthood

How do we face barriers to consolidating identity? Is coming out the same as other disclosures? How do we respond to disability?

Lessons for understanding adult sexual identity: Sexual identity is based on the consistent attraction of people to each other's sexual thoughts, fantasies, behaviour and lifestyle. These components may be compatible during some periods of our life, and contradictory and inconsistent at other times. We need to recognise these different parts of who we are as sexual beings if we want to integrate and consolidate our sexual identity.

The late South African pop singer and known bisexual Brenda Fassie once said: '*I am a big star. The world, black and white, is fascinated by me. Madonna is only big within white pop. I am beyond pop. I am life...*' ... Youth and adults may have similar needs when grappling with finding the appropriate moment to begin or continue their path of personal disclosure... People living with disabilities have the same needs as all other people when exploring and understanding their sexuality, finding supportive peers, grappling with coming-out issues, and getting access to accurate information and resources... In this section we also explore more examples of sexual diversity. These often occur during adulthood, but can just as easily develop... during other stages of our life, such as early or late adolescence... We will learn about six examples: Transsexual individuals, transgender individuals, intersexed individuals, effeminate males and masculine females, cross-dressers, drag queens and drag kings.

8. Responding to sexual diversity at school

How can we plan how we respond to sexual diversity? How can we creatively build safer schools? How can we develop challenging activities?

To be more effective in engaging with sexual diversity, we need to travel beyond preparing ourselves individually. We also should try to identify role players like the Department of Education, the school governing body, parents, the principal, other educators and staff in the school, your own learners and other learners in the school. ...

Martin Luther King once said: 'Everything that we see is a shadow cast by that which we do not see.' ... Strategies for including sexual diversity in safer schools – For schools: Have clear anti-discrimination policies that deal with homophobic bullying... Welcome and support lesbian, gay and bisexual learners, staff and parents. – For staff: Recognise and deal effectively with homophobia... integrate lesbian, gay and bisexual people throughout the curriculum. – For learners: Clear guidelines on acceptable behaviour... someone to listen to and take their concerns seriously... appropriate role models and stories of lesbian, gay and bisexual people, past and present, alongside positive images of people from other groups historically discriminated against (e.g. women, black people, people with disabilities, people living with HIV...).

* * *

The Educators Awareness Project (EAP) is still young and not enough practical experience has been collected yet. Only five workshops have been held, each with about ten teachers. The following points arose:

- Our approach might be too reliant on being pro-active, meaning that we need highly motivated teachers to want such a course. For them it seems to be very effective, but how to reach those who might need such training even more?

- How to develop a closer cooperation with and support from the Department of Education? As proud as we were to receive independent funding, it might have worked better to have representatives of the department on board from the very beginning

■ Our approach is time consuming. Although everybody agrees that a change of attitude can't be achieved overnight it might be equally important to create easier and shorter (1-2 hour) introductions to get more teachers interested and motivated

■ The quality of training teachers in South Africa receive varies considerably. How do we tackle the basics of sexual diversity without also touching on better teaching skills in general?

■ The conditions under which schools operate also vary hugely. We have schools in privileged areas with classes of 25-30 and those in poor areas with up to 80 pupils per classroom. Over 40 per cent of South Africans still have to survive on incomes below subsistence level.

The Safe Spaces programme

The Triangle Project have put immense effort into developing an outreach presence through the Triangle Project's *safe spaces programme*. Safe Spaces are community based groups that provide LGBT with a safe environment within their own communities and public areas which aim to:

■ be informed about the Triangle Project's programme and service areas, and to make services more accessible through information provision, assistance with booking appointments, and provision of money to cover transport costs

■ build confidence in order to begin to challenge homophobia and prejudice and create a sense of community among LGBT people

■ distribute information, resources, organisational material and brochures and

■ organise programmes and projects, life skills workshops, discussion and related activities, based on a needs analysis of each individual group.

Each Safe Space meets once a week at times within targeted neighbourhoods in public areas such as libraries or community centres or in a home. If the venue charges a fee, the Triangle Project cover these costs and makes the necessary bookings. The meetings are facilitated by a Triangle Project outreach worker, and the participants determine the content of the meetings. Most group ideas for projects and events are centred around sports, like netball and soccer and beauty contests: most of these reinforce a cross-dresser or transgender identity as the visible gay identity in the townships. There is limited self-motivation for the development of new ideas for growth and development.

The Triangle Project assist these local Safe Spaces in organising workshops, learning how to apply for money or how to draw up a business plan. Where needed help is given to find safer homes to stay. To receive these services a person needs to be 18 years or older, or have written permission from a parent or a legal guardian. However, younger participants also use the outreach spaces from time to time and they often talk about negative experiences at schools, both related to peers and school staff.

The dreams of the Triangle Project for 2010 are to increase the number of outreach spaces and to link up with more youth and human rights organisations in townships, to give more courses on dealing with sexual diversity and to expand them for a wider range of service providers including schools, medical staff and police and to reach a better racial representation (50 per cent black, 25 per cent mixed heritage and 25 per cent white) within the organisation at all levels.

PS In early 2007 the National Department of Education in South Africa and two organisations representing the gay, lesbian, bisexual and transgender community in the Gauteng Province called *OUT* and the Gay and Lesbian Archive reached an agreement over a pilot project to include educational material about homosexuality in life orientation lessons. The material, still to be developed, will work against homophobia in schools. The decision whether to follow this agreement or not will be left to each province.

This chapter is based on interviews and further communication by Lutz van Dijk with Dawn Betteridge, executive director of the Triangle Project in Cape Town. We thank Karen Kraan, international consultant of the Schorer Foundation, Netherlands, for her participation and advice.

Notes

1   For more legal information see also the website of the Constitutional Court of South Africa: www.constitutionalcourt.org.za. Most quotations are from this source.

2   Statements by Judges Laurie Ackermann and Albie Sachs and legal definitions from: Leonard, Arthur S.: South Africa's Highest Court strikes down Sodomy Laws, New York Law School (website) 2004

3   All facts relating to the murder of Zoliswa Nkonyana are based on several South African newspaper articles, among them: Sunday News, February 19, 2006 and on international coverage like the one of Human Rights Watch, New York, March 3, 2006.

4   On July 8, 2007 two more lesbians were murdered in Meadowlands, Soweto: Sizakele Sigasa (34), a well-known outreach co-ordinator for Positive Women's Network (PWN) and her friend Salome Masooa (23), were violently assaulted and then shot – 'execution style', as the police reported. A survey with 1800 lesbians and gays in three South African provinces confirmed that 'discrimination and violence against sexual minorities is on the increase.' More visibility seems – in certain circumstances – to provoke more negative reactions.

5   All quotations are from the Workshop Manual *Understanding Sexual Diversity in the Classroom*, Triangle Project, Cape Town 2005, quoted with courtesy of Pink Triangle Project, Cape Town.

8

Challenging homophobia in conservative Canada: forming Alberta's first Gay/Straight Alliance

Darren E. Lund

Although it is easy to talk about promoting fairness, it can be difficult to stand up for what we as educators know is right. We know from daily observations and a growing body of research that students are often discriminated against on grounds of their sexual orientation or gender identity. This dangerous situation is well documented in US schools (Boshenek and Brown, 2001) and here in Canada (Grace and Wells, 2001; Pruegger and Kiely, 2002). When asked for their opinions on the current situation in schools, some lesbian, gay, bisexual, trans-gendered and transsexual (LGBTT) students in Calgary, Alberta reported that they 'did not think they could get any support from the school due to teachers who were homophobic and a school system reluctant to educate others on these issues' (Pruegger and Kiely, 2002, p29). I believe that many fair-minded teachers and students wishing to promote acceptance on this issue simply need a bit of encouragement to take the first steps.

The reluctance of many educators to address sexual orientation is understandable if you are living and teaching in a community with overt conservative values. Now imagine that your community is one associated with extremist views and actions, and that one of the politicians representing your city is a conservative Canadian politician named Stockwell Day. The former Alberta Conservative provincial cabinet minister was routinely in the news for his narrow views on homosexuality which are reported briefly below. Day stepped down after a brief and disastrous stint as national leader of the right-wing Canadian Alliance party and was recently appointed Minister of Public Safety in the newly elected Conservative federal government.

The experiences of educators and students in Canadian schools might offer some guidance. To inform this chapter I have spoken with fellow activists in this field as well as drawing on my experience of helping to form Alberta's first Gay Straight Alliance (GSA) programme in a high school in a relatively conservative community. A group of student and teacher activists in the small city of Red Deer, with a population of about 72,000, have been able to make a positive difference toward acceptance in their school and community in the face of considerable opposition. There are a number of other courageous students, teachers and educational leaders in many communities who are willing to take risks to ensure that schools are safer places for all students.

Stockwell Day and the central Alberta political context

As a member of the Alberta government representing Red Deer, Stockwell Day often sparked controversy in the local and national media with his narrow views on sexual orientation, among other issues. Day once revealed his homophobic views by mocking gays during a performance at a social function of the Progressive Conservative political party but his official actions were more telling. In one nationally reported incident, he tried in vain to block grant funding for a 1997 project of the Red Deer and District Museum and Archives because it included the experiences of gay Albertans. At the time he was Alberta's Provincial Treasurer. Day tried to justify his interference in grant funding to a *Red Deer Advocate* newspaper reporter in August 1997: 'They made a mistake in pursuing a project which purports to reflect the sexual choices of one per cent of the population.'

Day took a lead role in actively blocking the inclusion of sexual orientation into Alberta's human rights laws. He regularly perpetuated prejudice against gay people himself by linking paedophilia, a heinous crime most often committed by heterosexual men, with the legitimate political struggle for equal rights protection under the law (Kossowan, 1994). Day maintained that discrimination against gay people simply did not exist in Alberta, asserting to an *Advocate* reporter in May 1996, 'I'm so tired of dealing with a few scant, fabricated stories. It just is not happening.'

Alberta's rights laws were eventually changed to include sexual orientation (Caster, 1998) but only after a Supreme Court ruling and an expensive, losing legal battle with a college instructor, Delwin Vriend, who was fired from the Christian institution for being gay. Another ultra-conservative Red Deer politician, Victor Doerksen, introduced a private member's bill on same-sex marriage. A law was passed in Alberta in 2000 that mandated Alberta to invoke the notorious 'notwithstanding clause'. The clause bypasses the protection offered by the *Canadian Charter of Rights and Freedoms* on the issue of marriage equality.

Promoting diversity in a conservative climate

In a political context such as that in central Alberta a voluntary student group formed to promote diversity in schools and society might expect to face problems. Surprisingly, this was not the case for our student activist group. Formed in 1987 by accident in one of my grade 10 English classes, the Students and Teachers Opposing Prejudice (STOP) programme thrived in a Red Deer high school for nearly two decades with the goal of creating an atmosphere of accepting differences. It attracted much media attention, no doubt because of Central Alberta's unfortunate reputation for extremist hate group activity (Kinsella, 2001). STOP received a 2001 Award of Distinction from the Canadian Race Relations Foundation and other regional and national honours for its work in countering discrimination (Alberta Human Rights Commission, 2000; Canadian Race Relations Foundation, 2001).

The STOP programme has organised activities including awareness campaigns on First Nations issues and violence against women, presentations to government officials, drama presentations to children, local protests, international human rights advocacy, public debates with political leaders on government policies and a variety of other projects (Lund, 1998). Each of these initiatives has involved students and teachers working together to tackle contentious issues on social justice themes. On occasion the group and its organisers have met with strong expressions of hatred (Lund, 2003). When we began our project to promote acceptance on issues of sexual orientation and gender identity, members of STOP were concerned that raising awareness about homophobia would be an overwhelming task.

Although the high school community had come to embrace STOP's antiracist messages, one of my colleagues and a STOP co-advisor, Kirsten Spackman, observed that she felt that the school was not yet a healthy place for some students:

> The school was not a safe environment for homosexual or perceived homosexual students. And by this I don't mean physically dangerous- although I know of one incident where a boy was assaulted at the downtown bus stop-but instead, emotionally and mentally torturous. Students frequently used degrading language such as 'fag' and 'dyke' and calling negative things 'gay.' As well, the most hurtful male insults attacked their sexuality. This created an environment of fear among students who were gay or even perceived to be gay.

Sadly, this is a fairly common occurrence in Canadian schools; for all the gains that have been made in eliminating racist slurs from the public discourse, derogatory comments against the LGBTT community are commonplace in most of the school hallways I have visited across Canada in recent years.

Raising awareness and acceptance of sexual orientation

Late in the 1999-2000 school year two conversations initiated a new activist group's formation in our high school. A student in grade 11 – let's call her Rebecca – approached me to ask why the STOP group did not do more to counter prejudice based on sexual orientation. I encouraged her to approach the STOP group. At the same time one of the school administrators raised her concerns with me about the increasingly dangerous situation for LGBTT students in our school. Events came together in June 2000 when members of STOP decided unanimously to form a Gay/Straight Alliance (GSA) committee, the first ever such group in Alberta. First they sought the principal's approval and then they sent out a call for student volunteers. Meeting once a week and organised mainly by students, the GSA was intended to deal specifically with reducing the discrimination faced by students on the basis of sexual orientation and gender identity.

Rebecca remembers that the school could be a cruel place for particular students in her peer group and talks about her reasons for wishing to form the GSA group:

> I do remember it was fuelled in particular when I discovered that my gay friend, Tim, was being harassed about his sexuality, and the counsellor who was supposed to deal with it simply didn't. I remember he said something along the lines of 'If Tim would 'flaunt' his sexuality less, he would be harassed less' as though it was Tim's fault that he was being harassed and his sole responsibility to stop the bullying. I was totally outraged by this response. The GSA, in the beginning, was a response or protest to this teacher's attitude. Also, I was interested in sexuality, human rights and gender issues, and I hoped that all of these issues could be addressed within the GSA.

Surprisingly, there was little initial backlash to the group in the large high school (which had a population of about 1800 students) or in the Central Alberta community. Even a front page newspaper story on the group in the *Red Deer Advocate* (Kennedy, 2000) did not elicit a single negative reaction from the community. My colleague, Kirsten, now remarks that 'our group has experienced remarkably little resistance or hostility from the school and community,' which she attributes to the careful groundwork laid by student leaders. Kristen and I were two straight allies who wanted to learn the best way to help our students organise effective school efforts to challenge homophobia.

Early in the GSA group's existence one of its student members – call him Roberto – had the courage to volunteer to address a staff meeting of about 150 adults, at which he offered a moving and poignant account of growing up gay in Central Alberta. He explained his fear of the violence that would come from his being exposed as a gay teenager and talked about the important role that teachers can play in fostering acceptance in schools. He asked the audience to help him and the GSA help make the school a safer place for all students. I remember him receiving the first standing ovation I have ever seen at a staff meeting.

Kirsten reflects on Roberto's courageous comments and the lasting effect that she thinks he had on the staff:

> One of our more confident students spoke with staff about his ex-periences in school. He actually came out to staff, which was a surprise because we didn't ask any of the students about their orientation. He finished his speech by imploring staff to do something about the problem because he just didn't want to be afraid anymore. The staff applauded a long time and understood, I think, how important their role was in engag-ing students who were using discriminatory language in their classes.

Other GSA members took care to get school administration and staff on their side from the outset, seeking the principal's approval before making any plans. As Rebecca recalls, 'I didn't think that it would be approved by the school – that was a surprise. I really hoped that it would start people discussing sexuality and diversity.' Student members regularly reminded staff and their fellow students that they were not a 'sexuality' club or a support group but a collective of students striving to create a safe and respectful learning environment. When she was asked how important it was to have teachers involved in the formation of the GSA committee, Rebecca answered:

> It was very important. I couldn't and wouldn't have done it with out the help and encouragement of you and Ms. Spackman. That support was necessary for both practical and emotional reasons. It also helped to know that other staff members were supportive of the idea, if not directly involved.

Some of the activities to raise awareness in the school were provoca-tive: the GSA group organised a Sexual Orientation Awareness and Acceptance Week in 2002 that featured a poster campaign with posters offering thought provoking messages such as 'Closets are for clothes,' 'Why do you care who I love?' and 'I don't care whether you're gay, straight or Australian.' Some of the posters were torn down but GSA members strongly suspected that just a small number of students were to blame.

During the GSA's second year of existence members drafted a formal looking and oversized GSA Declaration of Acceptance to model the Canadian Charter of Rights and Freedoms and displayed it by the school library during lunch hours. About 200 students and staff signed the declaration, promising to refrain from using derogatory language which was related to sexual orientation. The document was framed and displayed in a prominent position in the school. STOP members gave a rainbow ribbon to each person who signed the declaration to wear it during the week to signify their commitment to GSA's ideals.

Other ongoing activities have helped the GSA group to promote an atmosphere of acceptance in the school. Facts and myths about sexual orientation were included in the student bulletin at regular intervals. One lunch hour saw a local guest speaker, a protestant pastor from a popular local church, offer a bible-based talk on homosexuality to dozens of staff and students. He facilitated a discussion of sexual orientation from a Christian perspective that was neither hateful nor condemning.

On a designated Day of Silence, about twenty students refrained from speaking for the entire day to symbolise the silence surrounding the issue of discrimination against people because of their sexual orientation. They had prepared printed cards with information about the activity to give to their teachers or any students who asked them about it. Rebecca emphasises that the protection of the dignity of every student is a basic human rights issue:

> I think the most important argument [for forming a GSA] is taken from a human rights standpoint. The fact is that queer students are being harassed and marginalised in the public school system and by their peers and that's totally a violation of their rights. I think schools have a responsibility to protect and empower all students and, as much as possible, to create an environment that is safe, comfortable, and based on the idea of respect and dignity for all. Encouraging queer students to keep their sexuality quiet, even if it is in a subtle or indirect way, violates their right to express a fundamental aspect of their identity and beliefs.

Another group of students produced a haunting audio recording featuring historical moments of hatred, including the Nazis' treatment of the Jews, and the civil rights struggles in the US. The tape ended with a scenario involving the all too common expressions of hatred toward homosexuals, and issued a strong challenge to encourage young people to make positive choices in their treatment of others. The recording was played for the entire staff over the school intercom and copies were available as a resource for teachers who wanted to address these and other discrimination issues in their classes.

When asked if typical bullying programmes might be implemented to address the discrimination faced by LGBTT students in our schools, the students and teacher I spoke to were adamant that these programmes were inadequate. As Kirsten explained, there were specific reasons why general anti-violence initiatives do not deal effectively with homophobia:

> Everyone can agree in principle that violence and bullying are wrong. You won't however, get the same consensus about homosexuality. There are many people who consider homosexuality a disease, an abomination and even a criminal act. It is, therefore, very different. Adults in the community who say they don't support bullying may support anti-gay sentiments. It becomes necessary, then, for the school community to make it clear that even if a person disagrees with a particular belief that she or he has no right to take away that person's ability to feel safe in the school environment. As well, there are a whole series of myths that travel around about homosexuality that involve a whole different approach to awareness.

On the same topic, an activist student who recently graduated from a high school in Calgary, expressed the view that:

> Traditional anti-violence and anti-bullying programmes are not enough in schools because they are too simplistic. The issues behind, or motivating the bullying – homophobia, racism, etc. – are never addressed. The anti-bullying programmes that were presented when I was a student simply said that violence was bad and a cause of the perpetrator's low self-esteem. No discussion, no safe space, just end bullying.

A more comprehensive and specific programme of awareness raising and resistance is clearly needed in schools and the formation of a GSA can be an important first step in mobilising student activists and teachers to begin working together on approaches that will work best for each school context.

The work must continue

Central Alberta still has residents who hold narrow views about sexual orientation and there are still people who wish to deny human rights to certain groups of citizens based on their gender identity. Despite the best efforts of human rights supporters in the region there have been many examples of homophobia in recent years. In 2002 the *Red Deer Advocate* chose to publish letters to the editor expressing extremist views against homosexuality. However, following the resolution of a human rights complaint against them, the newspaper now includes a statement on their Letters page that reads:

> The *Advocate* will not publish statements that indicate unlawful discrimination or intent to discriminate against a person or class of persons, or are likely to expose people to hatred or contempt because of ... sexual orientation.

I have personally been subjected to hate mail and job threats because of my work on diversity issues (Knapp, 2006). In the past four years I have been the target of costly legal action, namely a $400,000 nuisance defamation lawsuit that was subsequently dropped, that I believe was designed to intimidate me into no longer supporting the fair treatment of gay, lesbian, bisexual and trans-gendered students. Another more violent reminder of the dangers of hatred came in the form of a vicious attack on a Red Deer teenager in July 2002 (Zielinsky, 2002). The victim, a 17 year-old male, was attacked by a man who used derogatory slurs against his perceived sexual orientation, asking him, 'You're a faggot, right?' before shattering his cheekbone.

Teachers and students in Alberta are fortunate to be supported by a forward thinking Alberta Teachers' Association (ATA) that provides a number of materials on teaching about sexual orientation and other matters relating to promoting fairness in public schools. Numerous resources are available free of charge online (ATA, 2006). Their Diversity, Equity and Human Rights web page includes teaching materials, a newsletter, workshop information, relevant publications, videos and media resources and an annual grant programme supporting diversity efforts in schools in Alberta. A booklet entitled *Safe and Caring Schools for Lesbian and Gay Youth*, also published by the ATA, is especially helpful. I strongly encourage teachers, parents and students to check with their local teachers' association and community groups for relevant policy, curricular and pro-gramme materials on this and other diversity issues.

As Rebecca points out, bringing up these issues appropriately with young people, either in a GSA or with the larger student body, is a challenging and complex task given the pervasiveness of homo-phobia in the larger community. She recognises that 'all students need to be told that they cannot harass or bully queer students, even if they seem to have the larger population backing them up in their behaviour.' However, she acknowledges that this means:

> dealing with the sometimes touchy subject of sexuality. I think that many high school students, even the straight ones, are not sure of themselves as sexual people and so the question of homosexuality is not going to be entirely easy or comfortable for them to talk about.

She recommends overcoming this discomfort for the safety and dig-nity of all staff and students. My GSA staff co-advisor, Kirsten, offers this advice for dealing with those who may oppose addressing these issues in schools:

> The best arguments are the ones that are personal. A person would find it difficult to argue with someone who honestly and emotionally tells a story of harassment. Avoid arguments that deal with whether or not homosexuality is wrong and stick with the point that discriminating against and harassing homosexuals is wrong.

Conclusion

While not everyone is expected to share the same ideas or opinions on controversial matters surrounding sexual orientation and gender identity, we can all agree that our public schools should be safe places for all students to learn in. Kirsten remembers having both hopes and fears when we first started the GSA: 'I had great hopes that we might be able to educate people about the hurtfulness of discriminatory language and attitudes. I had some fears that some of the more adamant staff and students might be verbally and/or personally abusive.' I am pleased to report that her hopes came to fruition and her fears did not materialise, and the GSA thrived for a few strong years in the high school where we both worked. Kirsten is now at another high school, working with a new student social justice group to address a range of diversity issues and I am working at university level to continue teaching, studying and fostering social justice activism in schools.

It is reassuring that my research reveals that many school-based activists continue their important work in the face of extremist backlash against diversity initiatives, a growing political and social conservatism and other potential inhibitors to social justice efforts. Keeping our focus on the goal of making schools safe learning environments will ensure that staff and student organisations and educational campaigns to challenge homophobia and promote the acceptance of differences will continue to flourish and spread to schools across our country and beyond.

Parts of this chapter originally appeared in Lund (2002, 2005) and are included here with the kind permission of the publishers. The author gratefully acknowledges the generous support of the Killam Trusts for this and other related work.

9

Governing bodies in Texas: talking about LGBT issues in the Christian heterosexual matrix

Michele Kahn

Homophobia in and outside education is a major problem throughout the USA. As this book was going to press, the Southern Poverty Law Center reported that seventy-five percent of gay students report being verbally abused at school, and more than a third say they are physically harassed (www.splc.org). Currently there are only nine states in the US with laws forbidding harassment based on sexual orientation in education, encouraging schools to provide a safer atmosphere (Safe Schools Coalition, 2004).

In certain areas of the country homophobia is especially pervasive. Texas, for example is a haven for conservative political, social and economic policies. As a result LGBT individuals are often excluded from basic civil rights such as marriage, protection from hate crimes, and surrogacy parenthood. These marginalising policies are usually framed in religious rhetoric and often mirror the attitudes of many of the education students who enroll in the required multicultural education course I teach at the university. This is problematic given that these individuals will eventually work in schools and will take with them their personal epistemologies that may then be reflected in school curricula and policies in the future. In this chapter I discuss how to approach LGBT issues in a conservative atmosphere by using strategies that focus on the construction of beliefs and empathic pedagogy.

The multicultural education course

I teach a required multicultural education course for graduate students who are studying for degrees in teaching, counselling or administration. Most of the students can be described as non-traditional. They are often older, having worked for some years and then returned to study for their advanced degrees. My classes tend to be large, sometimes with up to 40 students.

As part of the course requirements students write reflective responses and higher order thinking questions in relation to weekly readings and a cultural autobiography. They also present a group project and write a term paper. The course is structured around cultural attributes such as language, race or gender and then tied into how socialising agents such as school, church, or the family construct what it means to be Hispanic, female or having any other cultural attribute, and how this is reflected in school policies. Except for counselling courses, this is the only course in which students will read and discuss LGBT issues at length. These issues are introduced during the second half of the semester after discussion of gender.

Typically, a class starts off with small groups that are rotated throughout the semester where students discuss their reading reflections and questions. A whole group discussion, other activities, films and mini lectures usually follow. For most of the class period students are required to be actively engaged in some sort of conversation or activity related to the topic discussed. Throughout the semester, students present on various topics ranging from 'The construction of gender' to 'Bi-racial children and schooling'. The last two classes are devoted to a peer review writing workshop where they read each other's papers and have panel presentations, where they have two to three minutes to give a synopsis of their selected topic.

This chapter first describes policies in Texas relating to LGBT issues to provide background information which helps explain some of the conservative ideologies that students bring to the course. It then considers belief construction and empathic pedagogy, and concludes with specific recommendations on how to approach LGBT issues in the classroom.

Texas politics

Texas presents special challenges for the sexual minority population in legal, economic, educational and social arenas and has actively engaged in passing measures that discriminate against sexual minorities. As in several other conservative states in the USA, marriage is now officially defined as a bond between one man and one woman. Texas law also bans any legal arrangements which are similar to marriage.

In 2003 Lawrence vs Texas, a case involving two men who were accused of breaking the state's same sex sodomy law was ruled unconstitutional by the US Supreme Court. Texas was only one of four states at the time that still had same sex sodomy laws. In 2005 the House of Representatives approved Texas Republican Representative Robert Talton's amendment to Senate Bill 6 that bans gay, lesbian, and bisexual individuals from becoming foster parents.

Texas anti-discrimination law addresses neither sexual orientation nor gender identity (Tex. Lab. Code § 21.051, 2002; Tex. Prop. Code § 301.021 *et seq.*, 2002) and nor do the safe school laws. In 2004 a federal court in Lubbock TX upheld a school's decision to refuse to promote a gay-straight alliance. The school claimed that members of the alliance sought to promote the group through fliers that contained websites offering information about sex and that this was against the school's abstinence-only policy. The group was denied meeting rights by both the superintendent and assistant superintendent (Caudillo v. Lubbock Independent School District)

Homophobia is also reflected in the Texas education curriculum. Texas state board of education member Terri Leo has successfully forced two of the largest textbook companies, Holt, Rinehart and Winston and Glencoe/McGraw-Hill to define marriage as a 'lifelong union' between a man and a woman, thus excluding same sex unions and adding a religious undertone to the wording in their health textbooks (CBS News, 2004). Leo's latest mission, also with religious undercurrents, is to make sure that biology texts accurately present weaknesses in the theory of evolution (Texas Education Agency, 2003).

The anti-LGBT policies in Texas have advanced notions that LGBT individuals are unfit to be parents, do not have stable relationships and do not deserve the same rights as other residents of the state. This means that LGBT individuals not only face coming to terms with who they are in a heterosexist society but must also deal with the additional burden of state sanctioned heterosexism which is based on questionable research and fundamentalist religious rhetoric.

The nature of belief

A belief reflects something that individuals know to be true. Whether something is actually true or not is inconsequential to the believers as they are already in a state of belief. Understanding how individuals arrive at their beliefs is important as it can help them to change. Charles Peirce (1877) described four ways in which people fix their beliefs: tenacity, *a priori*, authority and the scientific method. Tenacious individuals do not wish to explore other options and refuse to see fallacies in the premises which uphold their beliefs. Peirce (1877) comments:

> When an ostrich buries its head in the sand as danger approaches, it very likely takes the happiest course. It hides the danger, and then calmly says there is no danger; and, if it feels perfectly sure there is none, why should it raise its head to see? (p101)

The *a priori* method involves believing in what we are most inclined to agree with. In this sense individuals have the beliefs first and then find the premises, which they think support the beliefs. 'Intelligent Design', for example, is based on the assumption that there is a designer, one with purpose and intelligence, behind certain features of the universe (http://www.intelligentdesignnetwork.org/). Despite the fact that most of the scientific community views this concept as pseudoscience, proponents are still determined to gather evidence to support what they have *a priori* decided to believe.

Then there is the method of authority, often premised on fear, where beliefs are *de facto* accepted. During the Christian Inquisition of the Middle Ages, Pope Innocent III declared 'that anyone who attempted to construe a personal view of God which conflicted with Church dogma must be burned without pity' (Tomkins, 1981, p57). This is a prime example of instilling beliefs based on authority. In the same way those who believe propaganda that LGBT individuals do not make good parents are basing their beliefs on authority and nothing more. There is no scientific research to support their claims. Beliefs that stem from the scientific method are generated from questions and testable hypotheses. While the scientific method is not necessarily foolproof as it may involve elements of tenacity, authority and *a priori*, it does give the individual power and a method to explore certain beliefs. It also provides a framework for settling disputes. It is difficult, if not impossible, to have a productive discussion when two opposing beliefs are fixed in different ways. It is like arguing with the Ku Klux Klan using scientific data when quoting the Bible. There is no room for agreement. Scientific method involves a specific process which can be tested. It is arguably more rigorous than the other methods described and provides more opportunities for advancing or discrediting certain beliefs (Rudolph, 2005).

All beliefs are formed within grand narratives (Lyotard, 1979; Foucault, 1988). However, as individuals fix their beliefs, they rely on these hegemonic ideological structures that represent a juncture of knowledge and power relations. These structures shape discourse about LGBT individuals. Multicultural educators must deal with students' beliefs that have been formed within hegemonic norms of heterosexuality. There must be an interruption and destabilisation of what Judith Butler (1990) described as the heterosexual matrix, 'that grid of cultural intelligibility through which bodies, genders, and desires are naturalised' (p151). Much of the religious discourse I encounter from students is also tied into this matrix, resulting in an even more complex pattern where belief often hinges on authority, tenacity and *a priori* methods rather than the scientific method.

This, coupled with strong biblical beliefs, presents special challenges. How do educators approach students whose beliefs are anchored in authoritative biblical rhetoric? How should educators respond to students who believe that homosexuality is wrong because the Bible says so? I am tempted to ask students if they realise that the Bible has been interpreted and translated thousands of times, and to ask if they follow all that they believe this document is commanding, or just certain parts? I've resisted handing out a letter widely circulated on the Internet to Dr Laura Schlessinger (Mikkleson and Mikkleson, 2004) on the topic of the abomination of homosexuality according to the Bible. Among some of the questions the writer asks are:

> 'Lev. 25:44 states that I may indeed possess slaves, both male and female, provided they are purchased from neighbouring nations. A friend of mine claims that this applies to Mexicans, but not Canadians. Can you clarify? Why cannot I own Canadians?' (paragraph 6). And 'I would like to sell my daughter into slavery, as sanctioned in Exodus 21:7. In this day and age, what do you think would be a fair price for her?' (paragraph 4)

As tempting as this is, I know it would be considered offensive and drive students away. One way I have tried to approach this problem is to provide contradictory information in hopes of provoking what Pierce refers to as 'irritating doubt'. He identified this as essential in belief change:

> Doubt is an uneasy and dissatisfied state from which we struggle to free ourselves and pass into the state of belief; while the latter is a calm and satisfactory state which we do not wish to avoid, or to change to a belief in anything else. (1877, p99)

When individuals are confronted with contradictory information it seems counterintuitive that they would not re-evaluate their beliefs. However, some tenacious individuals simply choose not to incorporate new information into their belief systems because it is too inconvenient and troublesome to change what they believe.

Addressing LGBT issues needs to be about disrupting categories within a hegemonic heteronormative framework. This means going beyond telling students that LGBT individuals need to be protected from harassment because this could lead to their dropping out of school, resorting to drugs and alcohol and even to a higher suicide rate, and tackling the core problem which is in essence the same as other forms of prejudice (Williams *et al*, 2005). Students need to know that what they consider to be normal and right are socially constructed categories and therefore unstable, unfixed, and mutable.

A major obstacle to guiding students to deconstruct and see the power of socialising agents such as the media, churches and schools is that they are not in the habit of questioning the *status quo*, especially those cultural attributes in which they have special privileges such as being heterosexual, white and English speaking (McIntosh, 1988). By extension, students often come to my course unaware of their beliefs, reminding me of a statement attributed to Margaret Mead, 'If a fish were an anthropologist, the last thing it would discover would be water'.

Before students can change their beliefs they must first acknowledge them. Students rarely come to my course believing they behave unfairly towards certain groups of people or hold unsubstantiated views of them. Frequently they are shocked to realise that the absence of LGBT issues in the curriculum is sexist and heterosexist. They are surprised to learn that most paedophiles are heterosexual males and that paedophilia is not a consequence of sexual orientation. Likewise, students show surprise when they realise how exclusionary and heterosexist some phrases such as mother and father versus care takers/guardians, and spouses versus partners, are to LGBT persons who are often parents, colleagues and students. There is a disconnect between what they think they believe and those behaviours they claim support their beliefs.

According to results of the Riddle Scale (Riddle, 1985), an attitude toward difference survey instrument, students typically reveal a *laissez-faire* attitude to homophobia. In the autumn semester of 2006 only thirteen students out of 43 in my class agreed with the statement 'It is important for me to stand up to those who demonstrate homophobic attitudes' and only six students agreed with statement 'It is important for me to examine my own attitudes so that I can actively support the struggle for equality that LGBT people have undertaken'. Surprisingly, 31 out of 43 agreed with 'LGBT people deserve the same rights and privileges as everybody else'. Students who disagreed with the first two statements and agreed with the last one appear to hold coexisting contradictory beliefs. I

117

struggle to understand how students make sense of agreeing with all of these statements yet not agreeing to examine their own attitudes and possible contribution to oppressive practices? somehow they ignore the anomaly: it does not irritate doubt and they remain unhampered by the contradictions.

Student attitudes and beliefs like these are problematic. Motivation and decision making issues have to be tackled if change is to take place. Too often, individuals who cling to homophobic beliefs tend to lack the motivation to look at different perspectives and individuals who feel that LGBT issues have nothing to do with their lives feel disconnected from such issues. Those who believe that sexual identity is only part of the home and not of the community need to redefine their family and community values. Students need to explore their own subjectivity and realise that they are active agents in how they construct themselves and others. This is where empathic pedagogy can help individuals to redefine how they see others.

Empathic pedagogy

I have read hundreds of the cultural autobiographies that students are required to write for the multicultural education course in which they often share life-changing experiences which have changed their deep-seated beliefs. Typically, students who have held negative feelings toward LGBT individuals admit to changing after developing a close friendship with someone who identifies as LGBT. Once the friend is out about his or her sexual orientation, the individual is forced to reconsider how he or she views LGBT people because of the empathetic feelings already established in the relationship.

Empathy is a powerful motivator: in its most extreme form individuals such as Mother Teresa, Mahatma Gandhi and the Dalai Lama have dedicated their lives to improve human conditions. Likewise, heroic individuals such as those in the aftermath of 9/11 or people who become part of relief organisations have dedicated their time, energy, resources and sometimes lives to helping others. What would it be like if every teacher, administrator or counsellor in every school had empathic skills which were strong enough to do whatever was needed to improve the conditions of their students. What would schools look like?

The literature on empathy is abundant as well as its definitions. Carl Rogers (1980) describes empathy as:

> ... entering the private perceptual world of the other and becoming thoroughly at home in it....To be with another in this way means that for the time being, you lay aside your own views and values in order to enter another's world without prejudice (p142-143).

Eisenberg and Fabes (1998) define empathy as:

> an affective response that stems from the apprehension or comprehension of another's emotional state or condition and is similar to what the other person is feeling or would be expected to feel. (p702).

They differentiate this from sympathy where sympathy is an emotional response stemming from the apprehension of another's emotional state or condition that is not the same as the other's state or condition but consists of feelings of sorrow or concern for the other (p75).

The primary difference between the empathy and sympathy is that someone who is feeling empathy is embodying what they perceive the other person is feeling whereas someone who is feeling sympathy is feeling concern, but not the *feeling* that he or she is perceiving what the other person is feeling. For the purposes of this chapter empathy is defined as the ability to feel and understand what another person is feeling, as well as being able to communicate the experience.

Empathic feelings can have positive effects. Empathy instruction leads to improved teamwork, greater job satisfaction, personal openness and mindfulness of others' needs in conflict situations (Cotton, 2001). Empathy can also create a desire to help others and can produce pro-social behavior (Sturmer, Synder and Omoto, 2005). The degree to which people treat each other with care and respect depends on the degree to which they perceive similarities between themselves and others, which is a central component in empathy (Levy, Freitas and Salovey, 2002).

Empathy must be taught in the multicultural classroom. Students left to their own devices may avoid empathic feelings since they are not necessarily pleasant (Jeff, 2004). Feeling empathy can also produce guilt, which can make students defensive and enter into a state of denial of another person's feelings. This often happens when I discuss white privilege in a classroom dominated by white students. Students are usually horrified at the idea that they may have reaped economical and social rewards at the expense of others. It's difficult for them to acknowledge and accept that they, consciously or unconsciously, play a role in oppressive practices and some students find relief for their feelings in denying that this privilege exists. Denial continues until they can find a parallel experience where they have been denied advantages: in this way they can connect with their role in white privilege.

Empathy instruction in the diversity course is also necessary because students need help making connections. They often do not see the similarities among themselves and as an instructor it is important to facilitate this process. One study between group membership and pro-social behavior demonstrated that people tend to help in-group members because of their identification with them but helping out-group members required some sort of interpersonal attraction in the form of physical attractiveness, dress, appearance, interpersonal behaviour or intellectual qualities (Sturmer, Synder and Omoto, 2005). To develop future educational leaders who can go beyond their local identities, we need to assist students in reframing how they view other groups of people.

Empathy development should focus on cognitive, emotional and communicative dimensions. Cognitively speaking, students need information to know that different perspectives exist and this information should be connected to their lives in some way so that they feel it. Just as importantly, the ability to communicate these feelings clearly demonstrates their existence. For communicative purposes, does it really matter whether we empathise if we cannot convey our thoughts?

Teaching empathy to students who want to become part of the educational system is essential because they will have daily and intimate contact with children who are learning about who they are and who they want to become. Considering that staff in the school system barely reflect the growing diversity in the student population, it is essential to have teachers, counsellors and administrators who can relate to their students and who know how to connect with them and want to do so.

Classroom applications

Creating a course which is conducive to students developing an open mind about LGBT issues requires certain processes to be implemented throughout the course, not only when LGBT issues are discussed. While these processes do not guarantee that every student who is prejudiced against LGBT will change, students can at least examine the heterosexual hegemony within which they live.

I therefore describe practices which are inspired by Peirce's (1877) ways of fixating belief, empathic pedagogy, as well as my experience as an educator and student responses. These strategies are based on the idea that fixation of belief and empathy can influence each other and offer a broader range of ways in which students can access different perspectives. The first part describes general characteristics that the multicultural classroom should have to create the conditions necessary for students to approach LGBT issues with an open mind. In the second part I describe specific strategies and activities that have been helpful when introducing LGBT issues.

General characteristics

1. Activities that draw out existing beliefs and experiences

Every class period should require students to reflect upon and answer questions related to their life as it is influenced by the larger society. This creates a habit of enquiry and reflection and may include asking questions such as 'what assumptions were made about you this week?' 'were they accurate?' and 'why do you believe those assumptions were made?' Students may also bring their own questions which have been influenced by the readings. Good questions reflect thoughtfulness and insight. Bloom's taxonomy (1984) of higher order thinking can be a helpful guide for students to develop questions that synthesise, analyse and evaluate the material.

2. Experiences that connect students with each other and the teacher

Creating a community is essential to developing empathy skills. Students will be more likely to consider different viewpoints when they have developed meaningful relationships in the classroom. Short icebreakers, such as 'Find someone who...' or 'Two Lies, One Truth' will help students to learn each other's names as well as information about who they are. Small group work, where all students can voice their opinions about the class reading provide opportunities for them to make connections with each other. When group composition changes on a regular basis, students have the opportunity to meet and speak with everyone in the class. Instructors should develop rapport with students so they feel free to express their experiences in class. Writing personalised feedback as well as having one on one time with each student by circulating in the groups can help to develop trust.

3. *Opportunities to examine belief structures*
The cultural autobiography that students are assigned can have a major impact on them as they are asked to examine certain beliefs and practices. They are also asked to share a moment or episode of their choice with the class and while some share light moments, many share life-changing experiences they have had. Every semester at least one student discusses a major belief change such as growing up in a racist environment and later having an interracial relationship. This is powerful for not only the student who shares the experience but for the students who are listening.

4. *Research skills*
One of the first skills students learn in the course is how to find information and how to evaluate it. Typically, students go to the library for an informational session on how to use the library databases and then have a separate presentation on how to evaluate articles, internet sources and other records. This is essential for their final papers as well as for the arguments on various topics they present in class.

Strategies specific to LGBT issues
1. *Pose questions or defining situations that help students become aware of the beliefs they hold*
'Would you go to a physician whom you knew or believed to be gay or lesbian if the person had a different gender from you?', 'if this person had the same gender as you?', 'If not, why not?' or 'Would you wear a button that says: how dare you assume that I'm hetero-

sexual?', 'If not, why not?' (Health Services Technology/Assessment Texts, nd). Questions like these force students to examine their possible biases. By opening up a dialogue about these issues they can work out what they think.

2. *Addressing myths and stereotypes in depth*

Myths or stereotypes should be challenged with reliable sources. One of the most common myths is that gay men are paedophiles. It simply is not enough to state that over 90 per cent of child molesters are heterosexual men. Students need to find out why gay men are perceived this way. This involves talking about gender roles as well as sexual orientation. I usually give students a list of statements and they decide whether each one is true or false. They have time to think about each one and to discuss it in their groups.

3. *Draw on real people, real stories*

Many students have never met someone (at least not that they are aware of) who identifies as LGBT. When they find themselves in the same room as someone who is sharing that part of their cultural identity, the impact can be long lasting. One of my guest speakers who spoke at length about the harassment she faced at school and the physical violence she endured, touched many students in my class. Another later shared the fact that her daughter had just come out and how her family was finding it difficult to adjust. Face-to-face meetings with people who tend to be perceived as different can be a powerful catalyst for empathetic feelings.

4. *Explore scenarios*

Students must practice how to talk about LGBT issues whether with children, parents, teachers or administrators. They should be given situations such as:

> A same sex couple with a child in your school has come to you complaining that there is a lack of literature with regard to kids with gay parents. How will you remedy this situation? What do you say?

> Or: One of your eighth graders recently confided in you that he/she thinks that he/she is gay. What is your next course of action? What do you say to the student?

Considering such incidents usually provokes heated discussions and confusion and provides perfect opportunities to address the students' construction of sexual orientation and its place in school.

5. *Differentiating between institutional and individual heterosexism*
Students must explore the normalisation of heterosexuality and the premises which claim to support it. I introduce them to the laws of the state and nation and they discuss the reasoning behind each. Students are asked to notice individual heterosexist behaviours such as assuming sexual orientation by asking a girl if she has a boyfriend or assuming that kids at school have a mother and father. One way to help them to think about this is to ask them to imagine what types of behaviours they would have to be aware of to hide their true identity if they were gay or lesbian. Another useful tool is *The Heterosexual Questionnaire* which asks questions normally asked of sexual minorities such as 'The great majority of child molesters are heterosexuals', 'Do you really consider it safe to expose your children to heterosexual teachers?' or 'What do you think has caused you to be heterosexual?' (Rochlin, 1977 in Back, 1985) Students usually find these questions ridiculous, which helps them realise how they have normalised heterosexuality.

6. *Examine information from various sources*
Students need to explore information from various perspectives and sources. They should receive statistical information about LGBT issues as they relate to all members of the community, including students, parents and colleagues. This should include approximate statistics of who is LGBT as well as what happens to students who identify as LGBT in school when these issues are not addressed. Historical information on the construction of sexuality and gender is essential so that students can see how perceptions change over time and place (eg same sex marriages in South Africa, same sex relationships in Ancient Greece, the Hijras of India). Students are also directed to read and discuss the American Psychological Association's resolutions on gay teachers, foster parents and students, as well as their statements condoning so-called reparative or transformative therapy as usually advocated by faith-based organisations such as Exodus International.

7. *Films*

Students need to see what schools would look like with LGBT matters incorporated into the curriculum. *It's Elementary*, a documentary that shows how different schools address sexual orientation never fails to impress students when they see openly gay teachers, schools having a gay pride day, or 4th graders discussing what gay means. There are other films teachers can consider such as *Adventures in the Gender Trade: A case for diversity, Because This is About Love: A Portrait of Gay and Lesbian Marriage, and Coming Out* (http://www.filmakers.com/GAY.html).

Conclusion

Belief and empathy are fundamental aspects of the way individuals construct their reality. They influence one another because empathy can be a catalyst for the re-examination of beliefs, and beliefs shape how we view others. By analysing how people come to believe, as well as capitalising on the power of empathy to elicit the desire to take action against oppression, instructors can create classroom conditions that provoke students to re-evaluate and reconstruct their beliefs about sexual orientation. Essential to the process is developing the habit of self-examination and taking different viewpoints.

Sections of this chapter have appeared in Kahn, M. (2006) Conservative Christian teachers: Possible consequences for lesbian, gay, and bisexual youth. *Intercultural Education* 17(4), p359-372.

10

The challenge of the white male heterosexual: dealing with resistance to queer studies in the ethnic studies classroom

Melinda L. de Jesús

Context

The 2000 US Census found that Asian Americans are one of the fastest growing ethnic groups in the country. Asian Americans now total 10.2 million and make up 4 per cent of the total US population, up 48 per cent since 1990. Chinese Americans are the largest subgroup (2.4 million), followed by Filipino Americans (1.9 million). Now numbering over 1.6 million, the Asian Indian population in the US has increased 106 per cent since the 1990 census. The Vietnamese American community has also demonstrated a growth spurt, increasing 83 per cent in the past decade (Asia Source Special Report: Asian Americans and the Census 2000 Results http://www.asiasource.org/news/at_mp_02.cfm?newsid=53011).

These numbers highlight the exponential growth of Asian American communities throughout the US, and correlate with increased demands for the inclusion of Asian American history and culture in kindergarten through 12th grade, as well as higher education curricula. But this struggle goes back more than 40 years: Asian American

Studies as a discipline was founded alongside African American, Chicano/Latino, and American Indian Studies during the 1968 Third World Student Strikes at San Francisco State (Louie and Omatsu, 2001). Ethnic studies have made strong inroads in redefining contemporary conceptions of what comprises American history and culture; nevertheless, scholars and activists doing feminist and queer work in this field continue to face strong resistance from patriarchal, homophobic, cultural nationalists who desire to silence or ignore the experiences of feminist and queer folks of colour in the name of racial solidarity.

To compound this issue scholars engaging in examinations of race, gender, class and sexuality have been singled out as targets by conservative watch dog groups like CampusWatch.org and Students forAcademicFreedom.org. These organisations maintain that classes focusing on analyses of privilege and power, particularly around race, gender and sexuality, amount to nothing more than 'political indoctrination' which threatens the white, heteropatriarchal *status quo.* Members of the faculty who teach these courses are deemed activist, liberal and biased and become targets for monitoring, subject to calls for removal or censure. One particularly egregious example of this is www.uclaprofs.com, a website created by a UCLA alumnus which lists 'The Dirty Thirty' UCLA professors who are deemed overly 'radical.'

Internal pressure in the form of homophobia within ethnic communities and ethnic studies combined with external pressure in the form of homophobic conservative groups threatening academic freedom ensure that integrating queer studies and ethnic studies remains a difficult yet worthy goal.

Introduction

From 1999-2005 I taught Asian Pacific American (APA) literature and culture at Arizona State University (ASU), a public, metropolitan university of over 60,000 students located in the US southwest. My students were largely from the midwest. Most were white and many were conservative Mormons. My time at ASU presented unique challenges related to the teaching of Asian Pacific American Studies, particularly my understanding of this discipline which emphasises the inter-related, competing and complex intersections of race, gender, class and sexuality .

As an ethnic studies professor teaching on a white majority campus I've become familiar with the vocal and defensive white male student who feels picked on when I lecture about institutional racism and white privilege. 'White guilt' often shuts down students as some feel implicated in or blamed for racist acts perpetrated before they were born. Furthermore, because Asian Pacific American studies seeks to center the voices and experiences of Asian Pacific Americans, some Euroamerican students, accustomed to the hegemonic privilege of their own history and world view, became uncomfortable.

As an Asian American pedagogue I found myself torn: I needed to deal with this student *angst* because I wanted all my students to be in a learning space, and also because I worried about evaluations of my teaching. I knew that many studies show that women and ethnic minorities get the worst teaching evaluations, but did my department chair and dean know this? At the same time I was saddened that my Asian American students had to listen to racist comments and resented having to spend so much time in the classroom managing white guilt and resistance.

Race was clearly a difficult issue for many of my students. However, I found it interesting that when I asked my classes to analyse race and gender/sexuality simultaneously, all of my students were most comfortable dealing with race in isolation. Overall, students felt that racial oppression was the most important issue and that attention to gender/sexuality competed too much with race issues. Furthermore, students readily grasped the concept of race as a social construct but failed to do the same for gender/sexuality. Students contended that homophobia wasn't a real issue because it was understood to be a 'lifestyle choice' whereas 'race cannot be hidden,' a particularly worrisome stance adopted by heterosexual students of colour. Sadly, because Asian Pacific American culture, like mainstream American culture itself, is homophobic, Asian Pacific American students are themselves often invested in homophobic ideologies. Osajima aptly describes their resistance in this way:

> ...teachers encounter resistance to learning when they want to develop an understanding of oppression and a commitment to social justice among students whose class, gender, ethnic or sexual orientation places them in positions of privilege. . ... Similar dynamics arise when. . . straights are presented with material on homosexuality and must confront their homophobia. (Osajima, 1998, p273)

To encourage all of my students to push through their discomfort and initial resistance, I emphasise the themes of coalition and compassion in the study of Asian Pacific American cultures, and work hard to help all of my students see themselves as allies for all members of the Asian Pacific American community because these are integral goals of the discipline itself. Osajima (1998) writes that Asian American studies classes help students 'become critically conscious of the multi-dimensional dynamics of oppression' (p 279). I ask my students, 'What's the point of doing antiracist work when a community itself remains homophobic and sexist?'

However, teaching diversity and advocating coalition on a white homogeneous, conservative campus like ASU translated into my own race/gender/sexuality becoming an issue. As a female professor of colour I embodied diversity itself and often students' anxiety about these issues was projected on to me. Moreover, my inclusion of queer art and culture in the course marked me queer by association because some students assumed that only queer folk would be interested in queer Asian Pacific American arts. My presence in the classroom and my courses could therefore be construed as challenging the mainstream *status quo*. Also, because the Phoenix area has a large Mormon population, the issue of conservative Christian views on homosexuality became an issue.

My case study of grappling with student resistance to studying queer Asian Pacific America follows. I analyse how one white male student, who felt his heterosexual privilege was being challenged in my classroom, attempted to discipline me personally rather than question the course assignments and topics. I reflect upon the impact this experience had on my pedagogy and my commitment to Asian Pacific American studies.

Case Study

I have taught Aspects of Asian American Culture over 20 times at three universities. This one semester course focuses on defining and exploring the parameters of the Asian Pacific American aesthetic as expressed in a diverse selection of cultural forms: theatre, fine art, literature, music, dance and film, as well as in the course subject matter. Queer and feminist arts are fully integrated into this curriculum, as it was designed to challenge the sexist and heterosexist biases in mainstream conceptions of Asian Pacific American culture. One required text is Diana Son's *RAW: Raunchy Asian Women*. This short explicit play describes the depths of four Asian American women's heartfelt desires for love, sex and acceptance. Three women are straight and one is a lesbian. Son employs a powerful, confrontational tone throughout to challenge the stereotypes of Asian-American women as either submissive, silent, docile lotus blossoms or erotic sex kittens and to centre the voices and experiences of real Asian American women. In the five years I taught this play at ASU most students initially expressed surprise and discomfort with the explicit language as they are required to present scenes from the play as readers' theatre in class, then usually designate this play the most memorable and challenging example of Asian American art in the course. However in Fall 2001, prior to my class's first session of readers' theatre, I received a copy of this email, sent to my dean, associate dean and dean's assistant:

> >Subject: URGENT: class monitoring required
> >Hello Professor,
> >I am student taking a class on Asian Pacific American Arts and Culture. I am requesting an immediate monitoring of APA 310 taught by Dr. Melinda De Jesus. [sic]
> The class in question has some subject matter that I feel is quite inappropriate for our university. The types [of] 'arts and culture' that are being taught to us have a very decidedly pro-feminist and pro-gay/pro-lesbian content, with very obscene language. Now I am not some bigot who is looking to have material I disapprove of removed from the university, however the material our instructor is providing has a very political agenda, which I feel is inappropriate.

>I am requesting that someone from your department (preferably a higher up) comes to observe our class on Monday 09/10/01 at 1:40PM in [my classroom].

It is very important to me and I feel others in the class as well that some person from the hierarchy from the College of Public Programs comes and observes the class.

The problem is that the class is being forced to act out Asian Pacific American plays with some very 'Raunchy' material. She could have easily picked some plays that are not nearly as offensive as she did, but this was not the case, I believe based on her personal politics. She is forcing us to act out these plays, and to many in our community, they would be considered obscene. I believe she would either give a degradation [sic] of grade to a student who disagrees with her views, or would be almost 'forced to resign' from her course. [sic]

I feel it is your duty to respond to this email with a presence in our class on Monday.

I really want to keep my anonymity. It will damage my reputation in class as well as in my personal life if it comes out that I wrote this letter. Please respect my privacy but just come view our class Monday at 1:40.

>Thank you for your time,
>Anonymous

I was stunned. As this was my web-based class, 'Anonymous' wasn't anonymous to me at all: I knew all my students' emails and URL's and now I would have to pretend that I didn't know the identity of the letter writer. I received the email from my dean about an hour before my next class meeting and though I was angry and upset I decided to begin class by telling my students about the email I had just been forwarded. I read them part of my dean's response, which was supportive:

Thank you for your inquiry regarding APA 310. Throughout Arizona State University, we value the importance of education, and here in the College [of Public Programs], we value constructive communication regarding pressing public issues.

If the course in question is bringing into the public arena issues with which you are uncomfortable, you could raise your questions about the feminist, gay/lesbian content in class – art and culture always have political implications, but some kinds of politics are more 'comfortable' than others! Or, you could schedule an appointment with the professor. Discuss with Dr. de Jesus your comfort level, and talk with her about approaches that will enhance your learning process.

We appreciate your interest in the university educational system, and if you would like to discuss this further, please contact the Associate Dean. For any classroom issues to be resolved, though, you will need to identify yourself.

I shared with my class that it upset and saddened me that they did not feel they could approach me about any issues they had with the required readings even though I had worked with them in small groups and no one had said anything. I again invited them to meet with me during my office hours. I reiterated to them that I had chosen plays by Diana Son, Jeannie Barroga, David Hwang and Wakako Yamauchi because they had been well received critically, were performed on college campuses and were regarded as innovative examples of Asian American theatre. Most of the class looked perplexed and concerned, and a few students, both Asian Pacific American and Euroamerican, spoke up, asserting that they were not upset about the choice and content of the plays we'd be performing. Class continued but Chymicalburn (the student in question) never once approached me to discuss his concerns and his presence in the classroom that semester made me feel very self-conscious.

A few weeks later I was given a copy of a letter written by Chymicalburn's mother about the same issues. Dissatisfied with my Dean's response (my programme and I were in the College of Public Programs), Mrs. Chymicalburn wrote a letter to the Dean of the College of Liberal Arts and Sciences and sent copies to the Chair of the Arizona Board of Regents, Arizona Governor Jane Hull, ASU President Lattie Coor, and *The Arizona Republic* (the local newspaper), in which she railed about my 'inappropriate' course content and also threatened to withhold donations to ASU:

There is not a chance I will ever donate to the school. I am disgusted and revolted by this situation. My son told me that he is enrolled in a course called 'Asian Studies' [sic] taught by a person [!] named Melinda de Jesus, who openly advocates to her students about her sexual preference (lesbian) and is having the class act out 'plays' advocating lesbianism. She refers to her class as a class on 'Queer Studies.' She is open about her dislike of males, and has not the focus in her class about learning Asian works in general, but Asian sexuality/lesbian issues. He asked someone from the department to visit the class, but was told that no one would visit because he would not disclose his name, fearing, of course reprisal in terms of grades. Do you not monitor class content and teaching at the school? Does anything go? Can anyone be hired to teach anything they want with no restrictions? If so, I am lodging a formal complaint to you about this method of education.Schools need to adhere to moral standards, community values, and the ethics of education... This is not education but exploitation and sensationalism. I want it to stop.

Clearly, for Chymicalburn and his mother, my incorporating feminist and queer-friendly aspects in my course automatically branded me a man-hating lesbian who foists her sexual preference upon hapless, powerless students. They put much effort into trying to discipline my presumably immoral sexual preferences, and my questionable course rationale. Because I had 'normalised' what should never be normal, they needed to reassert their world view and comfort level in my teaching space. Moreover, Chymicalburn had no problem demanding the imposition of his white male heterosexist vision of 'appropriate' Asian Pacific American arts and cultures onto my class, which told me a lot about his expectations of his own authority and privilege.

But would Chymicalburn have tried the same tactics with a white male professor? Was there something about my being an Asian American feminist, possibly a lesbian, that emboldened this student and his mother to resist my class and to try to discipline me so vigorously? Chymicalburn could have dropped my class but obviously wanted to stay for the fight because he needed to reestablish his world view in my classroom: a non-threatening, palatable Asian Pacific American studies for a homophobic, sexist, Christian, Euroamerican audience. I found this student's and his mother's actions incredibly disrespectful; and as an untenured junior faculty member

134

I was angry and extremely worried about how the entire incident would effect me professionally.

To their credit, my programme director and dean at the time backed me all the way. Their written response to Mrs.Chymicalburn affirmed my intellectual and pedagogical expertise. The dean re-assured me that this incident would have no affect on evaluations of my performance as an instructor. One important fact to note here, though: all the upper administration directly involved in responding to this incident were queer themselves, and all were strong campus advocates for feminist and queer studies, in addition to doing queer studies research themselves. I don't believe this to be the case throughout academia, though!

One 'out' was available to me: I could come out as a straight woman and thus deflect some of the accusations of queer bias in the class-room. But to me that was beside the point: did Mrs. Chymicalburn and her son intend to intimidate, shame and out me to my superiors and thus rid the university of my 'biased' queer pedagogy? My own sexuality had nothing to do with the inclusion of queer cultures in my classes and for this reason I was careful never to make comments about my sexual orientation. I rejected the simplistic idea that only queer faculty would use queer texts in their curriculum.

Another colleague, after hearing about this dilemma, asked me how I would 'make a safe space for that resistant Mormon student.' I im-mediately replied hotly that I would never want any student in my classroom to feel entitled and safe in his racist, homophobic, dis-respectful bubble. Later I wondered if my stance was wrong: as a teacher shouldn't I 'meet the students where they are?' Or was I wast-ing my time – was it even possible to reach students who were so narrow-minded and self-righteous?

After much soul searching I decided that because teaching Asian Pacific American Studies meant so much to me I had to refuse to compromise my personal, intellectual and political investment in this discipline by watering it down to make it more palatable for naive, threatened white students, and homophobic students of any race. I begin every course I teach by telling my students about the genesis of Asian American Studies in the Third World Student Strikes of 1968 and how Asian American college students put their lives and educations on the line to demand a curriculum that included their history and perspectives. I also tell my students that I teach to honour the memory of the brave undergraduates at the University of Vermont who went on a hunger strike for ethnic studies in 1996.[1] The activist basis of my discipline empowers me to maintain a strong stand for social justice in my own classroom and to demand respect for social justice from all my students.

I believe the Buddhist adage that 'when the student is ready the teacher appears'. Chymicalburn and his mother needed me to rock their worlds and I needed their fear and anger to refuel my dedication to a truly liberatory form of Asian Pacific American Studies. That semester I struggled to ignore Chymicalburn's passive-aggressive protests to focus on the rest of my students who were much more open-minded. In post-class interviews and anonymous evaluations they noted that the queer content of my class was appropriate for college level work: 'It's real life – and college is where we should be talking about this stuff.' And Asian Pacific American students reported that they were not shocked but surprised by its inclusion in the course for it offered a new way of thinking about the diversity of the issues Asian Pacific American communities face today, issues we are often unable to address.

Conclusions

The academy is not paradise. But learning is a place where paradise can be created. The classroom, with all its limitations, remains a location of possibility. In that field of possibility we have the opportunity to labour for freedom, to demand of ourselves and our comrades, an openness of mind and heart that allows us to face reality even as we collectively imagine ways to move beyond boundaries, to transgress. This is education as the practice of freedom. (hooks, 1994, p207)

I have argued elsewhere that Asian Pacific American Studies' investment in heteronormative, homophobic discourse only hurts us as a community, and that we need to employ more sophisticated analyses about the interconnections of race, gender, class and sexuality in our research and teaching (See de Jesús (2002) 'Rereading History/Rewriting Desire: Tracing Queerness' in Carlos Bulosan

America Is in the Heart (1973) and Bienvenido Santos' *Scent of Apples* (1979) and de Jesús (2000) 'A walkin' 'fo de (Rice) Kake: A Filipina American Feminist's Adventures in Academia'). However, I'm learning that it's one thing to research and write about these issues, it's another to teach them at a school like ASU. The intense resistance I experienced when doing queer studies at ASU, although it was from only one student, would make anyone wary of the consequences of including controversial texts in their teaching. Jettisoning all feminist and queer texts or films from my class would have been easy but would have severely compromised my political and intellectual investment in this discipline.

Luckily I had strong support from my college administration and colleagues and was not asked to do this. However, had I been employed at a different institution which embraces the more corporate-based model of university management which is more prevalent today, my dean could have regarded Chymicalburn and his mother as 'customers' who were dissatisfied with my 'product', and forced me to acquiesce to their demands to remove the 'offensive' content from my class. This reality has serious repercussions for all educators at all levels.

All teachers presenting anti-homophobic curricula face these issues at some level. I feel fortunate to be paid to read, teach and write about the topics I care about most and am grateful for the opportunity to integrate my political and spiritual commitments into my lifework. I'm thankful for each opportunity to reach one student who can then go on to reach her family, friends and co-workers. This is my vision of the transformative nature of education: each student I teach leaves my classroom more knowledgeable about Asian Pacific American history and struggles and has made connections to classmates and to communities they might not have known existed. My students become part of a struggle and a liberation movement that they cannot turn away from, and that gives me hope... which leads me to a final anecdote about this whole experience.

I had the opportunity to record an interview with Chymicalburn after the course ended, ostensibly to find out about student learning through web authoring. On tape he noted that initially the queer studies course content was 'so out there ... so open ... ' it seemed 'almost attacking' to straight Christian people like himself. However, he then related that my comments prefacing the final independent video we viewed for the class, Jennifer Phang's 'Love, Ltd.' (a farcical 'dramedy' about the silencing of queerness in Asian American families), really resonated with him. He recalled that I suggested that students who were uncomfortable about homosexual topics might think about the film this way: 'Twenty seven minutes of discomfort for you versus a lifetime of discomfort for Asian Americans who can't come out to their own families.' Although he never apologised nor identified himself to me, nor rescinded his or his mother's complaints to my dean and upper administration, by the end of the course even Chymicalburn understood why I needed to emphasise the cultural and sexual diversity of Asian Pacific America. And if *he* could grasp that, I believe that most students can.

Note

1   Judy Ashley's website ('History of Racism at the University of Vermont' <http://www.uvm.edu/~culture/uvm/>) details the history of the University of Vermont ALANA (Asian, Latino, African and Native American) students' struggle; my article, 'A walkin' 'fo de (Rice) Kake: A Filipina American Feminist's Adventures in Academia or, A Pinay's Progress,' describes my experience as a postdoc at UVM.

11

Surviving under pressure: working for 'Days of Tolerance' in Poland

Krzysztof Zablocki

Historical roots of homophobia in Poland

It is difficult to know where to start to discuss topics such as homophobia, confronting homophobia or working for Days of Tolerance in Poland today. It may be best to take a brief look at the current political situation. It does not seem terribly promising.

Poland has never been a modern, mature parliamentary democracy. Before World War II it was more an authoritarian semi-democracy. A true democratic political process started to evolve in 1989 after fifty years of political oppression. This oppression started in September 1939 with a tragic period of Nazi occupation, followed by a grim Stalinist period and more tolerable years of so-called 'real socialism'. Despite various moments of political, social and economic crisis, the period after 1989 initially produced an atmosphere of substantial freedom, tolerance and interpersonal kindness.

The situation changed in the autumn of 2005 when the PIS (*Prawo i Sprawiedliwosc* = Law and Justice political party) gained the largest number of votes in the Polish parliamentary elections. The PIS won a narrow victory but was unable to form a government on its own –

the number of votes obtained was well below 50 per cent. It felt that it nevertheless had a national mandate and that therefore its notion and policy of 'law and justice' should prevail. PIS is an overly 'patriotic' and xenophobic party, led by the Kaczynski (identical) twins, and drawing its electorate from the traditional but also less educated and economically dissatisfied strata of the population. The PIS formed a coalition with two rather exotic parties. One was the LPR (*Liga Polskich Rodzin* – Polish Families League), an extreme right wing party having its roots in several pre-second world war political parties, groups and organisations, which were xenophobic, anti-semitic and reeking with religiosity. The other was *Samoobrona* ('Self-Defence'), a populist, quasi-peasant party that has at least some roots in the Polish communist party and its political affiliates dating back to the period of the People's Republic of Poland. Due to controversies and constant internal friction, the coalition is fragile and vulnerable to dissolution.

The dominant political and social climate in Poland is certainly not conducive to openness and tolerance in the sphere of sexual orientation. But this is characteristic of Polish society in general. After the First World War, all articles in the penal code relating to 'non-standard' sexual activity were removed and homosexual or sodomist relations were not even mentioned. Thus, at the time, there was no legal basis for penalisation of homosexuality as was the case in Great Britain or Germany. And this continued after World War Two. So Poland has never officially penalised homosexual behaviour. But this does not mean that tolerance of homosexuality has ever been high. Poland is in some ways unique: it was at times more tolerant than western Europe in that no religious heretics were ever burnt at the stake but at the same time it has always been strongly Catholic, traditional, patriotic and even xenophobic. Patriotism and Catholicism have been two of the non-material imponderables which allowed the nation to preserve its identity against powerful historical and geopolitical force, so these qualities should not be lightly dismissed. In the twentieth century the most common attitude to homosexuality and homosexuals was simply to ignore them.

While Poland was a satellite of the Soviet Union homosexuals were not particularly targeted and there were numerous openly homosexual people in public life. Some of the major post-war Polish writers were homosexuals or lesbians and they did not try to hide their sexual orientation. Repression was never far away, however. In the mid 1980s *Hyacinth* aimed to register in police files all those suspected of a homosexual orientation. This infamous police operation blatantly violated human rights and created possibilities for future blackmail. The police also tried to induce many of the people they interrogated to become informers.

The transformation of the political system in 1989 did not bring about much change in official or general attitudes. It quickly became apparent that a large proportion of those protesting against the political system had been fighting for their own, traditional and Catholic-oriented, perception of freedom and had little interest in defending the rights of their LGBT fellow citizens. Europe, with its more liberal values, was treated with deep distrust.

Some fresh air since the 1990s

In spite of the generally unfavourable climate, gay and lesbian life really commenced and steadily developed during the early 1990s. Gay and lesbian societies were established and numerous pubs and clubs were opened in the big cities. Some became fashionable among straight young people as well: metrosexuality is the name of the game among younger people in Poland today. Twenty and thirty year-old gays somehow fit into this new sub-cultural phenomenon. A good many books on homosexual topics, both fiction and non-fiction, have been written, translated and published, numerous films have been shown in movie theatres or on TV and several plays have been staged. This has led to a certain de-exoticisation of the topic, especially among the younger generation. The changing climate has also led many more young people to take the risk of coming out to friends and family and not being rejected for this. Admitting to being gay or lesbian has ceased to be traumatic in some circles.

However, all attempts to go public with anti-homophobia campaigns in an open and visible way have met with sharp and violent counter-reactions. In 2004 the organisation *Kampania Przeciw Homofobii* (Campaign Against Homophobia) organised a poster campaign with large photographs of gay and lesbian couples placed on billboards. Attractive and casually dressed young people who looked mainstream were pictured, usually outdoors, with the slogan 'Let Them See Us'. For the more conservative elements of society this went too far. The image of two men holding hands was deemed 'perverse pornography' in the eyes of many.

The same response awaited the Equality Parades. The first Warsaw parade was organised in 2001, before the city was governed by right-wing hardliners. The parade, though less well attended than those in 2002 and 2003, was peaceful and the turnout increased steadily. But they were a far cry from the Gay Parades in the USA or western Europe. The Warsaw parades were rather timid demonstrations of mostly conventionally dressed people. Some participants did carry anti-homophobic signs and on occasion there were accompanying political protests. But in 2004 Lech Kaczynski, now the President of Poland, was the Mayor of Warsaw and the situation changed dramatically. Kaczynski openly declared that he would not permit the parade to take place. The argument with the organisers lasted for some time, with Kaczynski's officials continually introducing new bureaucratic obstacles which were later declared by the courts to be unlawful.

The 2004 parade was replaced by a rally in one of Warsaw's central squares. The turnout was impressive and the publicity enormous. The local authorities' aim to ban the march had backfired. The situation repeated itself in 2005 and 2006. The parade was declared illegal in 2005 but was held nevertheless and had a turnout of many thousands. Some participants were present to protest against the violation of citizens' rights to demonstrate. In June 2006, after a long period of uncertainty, the march was finally deemed legal. City authorities were forced to recognise that their position was untenable.

Other parades took place in Cracow and Poznan and in both these cities the situation became confrontational and even violent. In Cracow the participants were attacked with stones by extremist right-wing thugs in 2005. In Poznan, in the autumn of the same year, people were rounded up by the police and arrested in a violent manner. Later the court ruled that the banning of the Poznan demonstration by the city's president was unconstitutional.

The homophobia of governing politicians in present day Poland

The educational situation in Poland today reflects the general political one. The Polish Minister of Education, who is also a deputy Prime Minister, is Roman Giertych from the Polish Families League. Just after assuming his post, the Minister dismissed the director of the Centre for Teacher Training and Development because it had published a translation of a book approved and sponsored by the Council of Europe which presented ways of educating young people about human rights. The book included a short discussion on sexual orientation and suggested inviting a homosexual person to school to meet with the pupils. The book, although officially approved by the previous minister of the ruling PIS party six months earlier, was considered by Roman Giertych to be a textbook that promoted homosexuality.

Giertych has also suggested that Darwin's theory of evolution should be declared a hypothesis, presumably false. He further recommends that teachers be instructed to focus more on creationism. This is in line with the opinions of his father, Maciej Giertych, a professor of dendrology (Forest Sciences) and a Euro-deputy, who in recent years has started to propagate the idea in Poland and Brussels that Darwin's theory is false.

Two other prominent members of the LPR party have also recently spoken out in ways that give cause for concern. Wojciech Wierzejski, an MP and second in command to Giertych, has habitually reviled homosexuals in a primitive, vitriolic and offensive way. He refused to shake hands with Robert Biedron, president of the Campaign Against Homophobia and now a public figure in Poland. The reason for this public gesture was the fear of contracting an illness, presumably the HIV virus, by touching a gay person's hand. In the spring of 2006 Wierzejski and Giertych joined forces to advocate a ban on the Equality Parade. Wierzejski went further by suggesting that when dealing with such 'illegal' demonstrations by 'deviants', the police truncheon was the best remedy. Robert Wiechecki,

Minister for Maritime Industries, spoke publicly of homosexuality as a state of 'psychical and physical degradation'.

No tolerance for 'Days of Tolerance' in schools

In view of this growing intolerance in education the fate of the following two projects is not surprising. In early 2006 groups of politically active pupils in two secondary schools in Warsaw attempted to organise Days of Tolerance, to include discussions about the place of homosexuals in the public domain. In the first of these schools a planned meeting with Robert Biedron, president of the Campaign Against Homophobia, was called off at the last moment. The priest who was responsible for religious instruction in the school protested against holding a meeting with a gay person on Ash Wednesday. In the second school all the panel discussions were cancelled. However the Days of Tolerance discussions were held – but not on the school premises.

So what is to be done? Is the situation totally and irrevocably tragic and hopeless? Homophobia is a complex issue. It is manifested in different ways, from primitive hate-based attitudes, which are shared by leaders of the co-ruling LPR party, to less hateful but simplistic, outdated and intolerant views which are found among the majority of Polish government members and other civil service representatives. We also find a kind of enlightened homophobia among numerous people who are educated and perceive themselves to be liberal and tolerant. These liberal attitudes can be found among the leadership of the main opposition party, the PO (*Platforma Obywatelska* or 'the Citizens' Party'). While purporting to be tolerant and projecting a more urbane, civilised appearance, the leading politicians of this party think that matters relating to sex should not be 'manifested in the open' but remain locked in the proverbial closet.

Nevertheless, gay/queer life, despite all these setbacks, is alive and kicking in Poland: many young gays and lesbians, whether high school pupils or university students, who dare to come out belong to the more educated strata of the younger generation.

Fortunately, Poland is a member of the European Union, so the right-wing authorities, however disgusted and irritated by what they

144

see as the 'degeneration' of the liberal western part of Europe, cannot neglect the likely financial cost of an all-out assault on human rights.

In Poland's larger cities individuals can express their sexual orientation relatively freely. The situation is quite different in smaller towns and villages, where there is also more poverty. The fight against homophobia has a different character depending on where you are in Poland. A major step forward would be to treat non-conventional sexual orientations as alternative but perfectly normal whenever the subject is mentioned. This is how most of my gay friends in academia deal with it.

The opportunities are certainly more limited in secondary education. Pervasive pressure by the Catholic community, public opinion, priests responsible for religious instruction classes, parents, school directors and staff and even some of the pupils who belong to Catholic organisations do not give much breathing space. Looming over all of this is the menacing figure of the Education Minister, not only because of his views but also because of his immense height: he is about two metres tall and has a loud and domineering voice. The impact of Giertych's physical features is striking and underscores his hardline, off-putting ideological stance.

Teachers – gay or straight – as role models

We should never underestimate the impact a single teacher can have on students in spite of the socio-political ideas that prevail. There are various techniques which allow a teacher to bring up issues relating to gender, sexual orientation and generally LGBT and queer issues in Polish classrooms. These issues have no place in the official curricula of Polish schools but much depends on the teacher's intellect, learning, experience, empathy and good will. Teachers who are alone in the classroom with their pupils can exercise a fair amount of discretion to engage in a free exchange of ideas if they have the courage and skill to swim against the tide.

Homosexuality can be mentioned on many occasions when talking about literature or culture. So many great figures in world literature and culture were homosexuals and it is important to mention their orientation without ironic, sarcastic, knowing smiles. In a history class or when talking about political or social topics, teachers can mention gender or sexual orientation or human rights issues. This can be done at both the university level and in schools.

The choice of educational content also matters and academics are freer in their choices than the schoolteacher. When I teach elements of British and American culture at Warsaw University, I introduce my Cultural Studies class to topics like Shakespeare's sonnets and their translations into Polish, the trials and tribulations of Oscar Wilde, the idiosyncratic greatness of Quentin Crisp, the theatre of Joe Orton and the cinema of Derek Jarman. I discuss the issue of sexual diversity, so important in the lives of these people, as something quite normal, and I hope my students understand that being gay can be a source of pride rather than something to be ashamed of.

Schoolteachers or university lecturers who adopt this approach are doing something different from those who organise much publicised meetings with gay activists or lectures, conferences or workshops on gender, queer and human rights topics. These more visible activities do take place in our country and have been organised by various gay, lesbian and queer associations. They have been initiated both by major organisations, like the Campaign Against Homophobia and Lambda-Warszawa, as well as by smaller, local ones, sometimes affiliated to Arts/Social/Cultural Studies/Philosophy departments of the university[1].

Support from LGBT organisations

The association Lambda-Warszawa has been organising support and discussion groups for young people in Poland. The so-called Academic Group has focused especially but not only on university undergraduates. Participants meet once a week and discuss various topics, sometimes only loosely connected to LGBT issues. The aim is to strengthen mutual trust among the participants, who are all in the same boat. Sometimes close bonds of friendship are formed and some of these have resulted in partnerships.

Young people who have problems with accepting their orientation gradually realise that being gay is quite normal. This conviction is strengthened by the fact that most of the support group participants are intelligent, ambitious people who are successful in their studies. Sometimes group leaders are qualified psychologists.

In sum, a dynamic and sometimes contradictory situation has developed in Poland. Gay and lesbian activists have no access to schools and gay issues cannot be discussed in these institutions. But there is a need to address these issues. The Campaign Against Homophobia (www.kampania.org.pl) and Lambda-Warszawa (www.lambda.org.pl) carry out annual surveys on discrimination against gays, lesbians and bisexuals in Poland, and these results are published. The 2005/2006 report showed that more than half of those surveyed had experienced either physical or psychological violence in recent years. This is a serious matter. LGBT societies and activists are working to make existing problems visible and help those who experience psychological discomfort or who suffer from discrimination, abuse or physical violence in schools or in the workplace.

Though little can be done in schools in a structural sense, the wide-ranging activities of the LGBT community have certainly had some positive effects on the public mindset, especially on the younger generation. We need to realise that we have to take one step at a time.

Note

1   Important scholarly Queer Studies conferences have also been organised by the American Studies Center of Warsaw University and other academic centres. The efforts of Tomasz Basiuk, Dominika Ferens or Tomasz Sikora (who initiated Queer Conferences in Poland) and other scholars are impressive and so is the work of vigorous feminist organisations and groups with such public figures as Kinga Dunin, Agnieszka Graff, Kazimiera Szczuka and Magdalena Sroda. In Poland there is a strategic alliance between feminist and LGBT groups.

Starting with the initiative of young Polish teacher Marzanna Pogorzelska an open petition to Minister Giertych was published in July 2007 by a group of teachers and psychologists to raise more protest against his policy. This petition can be also internationally supported and signed online in Polish, English and German under: www.protestnauczycieli.pl

As this book was going to press, the Polish Education Ministry proposed a new law that would punish any teacher who mentioned that men can love men, or that women can love women, with redundancy and/or fines (the Editors).

Part 3
Examples of Best Practice

Lobbying for rights and protection

Barry van Driel

Target group: All levels of education

Subjects: Cross-curricular – all subjects where strategies for dealing with or eradicating bullying and discrimination are discussed

Focus: Activities designed to intervene and end oppression, harassment, bullying and discrimination through lobbying and collaboration.

Duration: days or months, even years

Materials needed: Network of stakeholders and organisations devoted to anti-discrimination work

Context: During the late 1990s a high school student in a Central California public school experienced frequent bullying. He attributed this to the fact that he dressed and behaved in an effeminate manner. He was not openly gay at the time. After a pattern of bullying had set in, his mother approached school and asked what action they would take to make her son feel safe there.

School reaction: The initial reply from the school was that there was little they could do. They advised her to tell her son to dress differently since his dress was seen as provocative and the cause of the problems. The school had a few openly gay teachers but they decided not to get involved.

A decision to confront the school: Both son and mother were dissatisfied with the response of the school which basically amounted to blaming the victim for his victimisation. They then contacted various social service organisations to ask what course of action they could take other than removing the boy from school for his own protection.

Several community social service representatives who were gay decided to put together a task force to put pressure on the school to take action. They confronted the school with a list of recommendations, including that:

■ all staff should receive training around GLBT issues

■ all staff should watch a video on this topic.

The task force gave the school two options:

■ Do nothing about the incident and recommendations. In this case, the task force would publish in the newspaper and elsewhere that the school had refused to take action to support students who are at risk

■ Implement the recommendations. In this case the task force would publish an article telling the community at large how the school had taken appropriate action and was a model of best practice.

The school, under significant pressure from the task force, reversed its stand and decided to implement the recommendations. Because the school took responsibility for the issue the climate has changed significantly.

I am indebted to Trevor Davis, Child Protective Services manager in Central California for this example.

Persecution of Homosexuals during World War II: the true Story of Stefan K. and Willi G

Lutz van Dijk

Target group: Ages 13-18 (all schools)

Subjects: Literature, History, Languages

Focus: Persecution of and discrimination against minorities in history. Homosexuals during World War Two

Duration: two lessons

Material: Youth literature – van Dijk, Lutz: *Damned Strong Love – the true story of Stefan K. und Willi G.*

Introduction for educators

Damned Strong Love was a collaborative effort between the author and the Polish gay survivor of Nazi persecution Stefan K. (pseudonym). The book was originally written in German and has been translated into English, Japanese and other languages.

In the book, Stefan K recalls his life as a young man in occupied Poland during the second world war. When the war began in 1939 he was 14 years old. At the age of 16 he fell in love with a German-Austrian soldier slightly older than he. He was arrested in 1942.

Stefan K was born in 1925 and died in 2003, aged 78, in Warsaw, Poland. His wish was to protect his full identity during his lifetime. Despite his wish for anonymity, Stefan K twice went on reading tours in the USA, giving witness at the Washington Holocaust Memorial Museum and at the Steven Spielberg Foundation in Los Angeles. In Europe he only gave public readings in the Netherlands. The book will be finally published in Polish in 2008 using his real and full name name – Stefan Teophil Kosinski – with his permission, which he gave before he died.

The lesson plans focus on what it means to develop and protect one's identity under life-threatening conditions. They pre-suppose a classroom where students feel safe and where controversial issues such as sexual attraction are discussed openly.

Lesson 1: Discrimination against Homosexuals in History – specifically the Nazi period

During the first lesson the students are asked:

- What do you know about Nazi Germany (besides the name Adolf Hitler)?

- Which groups were privileged and which discriminated against by the Nazis?

- Collect as much information as you can about the groups which were discriminated against and later persecuted and even murdered – what reasons were given? Were children and teenagers also persecuted?

- Find personal stories about the childhood and youth of some survivors from different groups such as Jews, Roma and Sinti (Gypsies), physically and mentally challenged disabled people, homosexuals and others

- Conduct the research in groups and report back to the class.

Lesson 2: Stand up for yourself – the gay survivor Stefan K.

Students read about Stefan's coming out to himself on his sixteenth birthday, after his older brother had confessed his desire for girls (p 35):

> What had formerly been strange and incomprehensible to me became clear all at once – I wasn't especially late or slow to develop. It simply had nothing to do with me – the jokes of the other boys, the silly fuss between grown-up women and men. It was all wrong – wrong for me...
>
> Everything that he'd told me so trustingly about girls, I felt exactly the same toward him. I saw how he closed his eyes ardently when he was at the high point of excitement. I also closed my eyes and saw him, my half naked, brave, reliable, loving, big brother Mikolai – this beautiful man.

Honestly, it wasn't cowardice that kept me from telling him then that I didn't dream of naked girls at all but of him. I was so simply overwhelmed that I didn't want to detract from this moment of enlightenment with ridiculous, stammering explanations. Besides, I had such boundless faith in Mikolai that I simply couldn't imagine that he would reject anything I felt.

- Remembering: Students are asked to write down how they felt the first time they became sexually attracted to another person of whatever sexual orientation. If a group is shy, the students can write notes without putting their names on them and later read the anonymous notes to each other

- Students are asked to reflect on the following questions: How does Mikolai feel about the object of his desire? What about Stefan? Why could it be important for the brothers to share their feelings with each other and not with other people like their mother? Does Mikolai feel guilty about his desire? Or Stefan about his? Students can do a role play in which a panel of experts that discuss these issues

- In groups, find out more about Stefan's life after 1945. Report back to the class.

Educational reflections on the lessons

The main purpose of these lessons is to be able to place discrimination against minorities in a historical context and to learn about how the Nazis discriminated specifically against homosexuals and certain other groups. In addition, there are several opportunities to feel at ease with Stefan's search for his sexual identity since most young people tend to be engaged in this quest. Questions are phrased in such a way that all the students can take part in the discussion on an equal footing.

Several school readings and follow-up discussions have shown that the space created for open discussion encouraged lesbian and gay learners to come out to their classes, sometimes immediately, sometimes after such a reading. In some cases discomfort about homosexual students or teachers was identified and strategies to address this were discussed.

Addressing lesbian, gay, bisexual and transgender equality in primary schools: books for use in primary and early years settings

Renée DePalma

Target group: Primary and early educational years

Subjects: Reading and writing, citizenship education

Focus: Normalising and mainstreaming GLBT issues in the early years

Duration: Several lessons to read and discuss books

This contribution is about some useful resources and not a specific lesson plan or exercise. At the first national meeting of the *No Outsiders* project, we each selected a book from our list and wrote a brief account of it. These are some of our selections:

And Tango Makes Three
Justin Richardson and Peter Parnell, New York: Simon and Schuster

(Warning: this book mentions snuggling...) This is a story about a zoo, about penguins, about how penguins raise their young. The thread that holds it together is the everyday warmth of a family and simple joys like feeding, swimming together, and (shhhhh) snuggling.

It just so happens that the parents in this story are both male; it just happens that their keeper was smart enough to notice that they were pairing; it just happens that the story is true, based on a pair of male penguins in Central Park Zoo who formed a bond, were offered an egg to foster and from that egg raised Tango. The two dad thing is almost an aside: the enduring and endearing core of this story is the everyday, practical childrearing love I would want for every child and every parent.

If my reading of *Tango* is anthropomorphic and idealises family, I certainly won't be alone. These are commonplace adult responses to stories written for young children and this is a normalising story of gay parenting. Bring on the snuggling!
Nick Givens, Regional Research Supervisor

Hello Sailor

Ingrid Godon and André Sollie, London: Macmillan Childrens

This is a delightful little story of love, lighthouses, and longing. Matt, the lighthouse keeper, has fallen in love with Sailor, who has gone off to sea as sailors are wont to do, leaving Matt with a promise that they will sail round the world together one day. He concentrates on keeping his light alive so that Sailor can find his way back. His friends Felix the postman and Rose are sceptical: 'I bet he's been swallowed by a whale. Or captured by pirates.' Matt is starting to ignore these friends as he longs for Sailor's return, but Emma writes to say that she is visiting tomorrow for Matt's birthday.

The party is a success, but though they buy rum for Sailor he does not appear. Matt is given a real sailor's jumper for when they sail away together.

Suspense sharpens, the colours darken, unfulfilled hope stretches. When the guests have gone and the light has dimmed, a man appears, walking over the sands to the lighthouse, calling for Matt. There is no answer against the wind. But then in the light of the lamp, the two meet again and 'the two friends didn't know whether to laugh or cry. They turned round in a circle to get a better look at one another. It was almost as if they were dancing.' Joy.

They escape together at dawn, leaving Rose and Felix with nothing but the dirty dishes, and eighty-three steps to climb to the top. The friends in turn start their waiting, waiting for Matt to come home.

This is not an explicitly gay love story, but it is a story of love and longing between two men, with immensely poignant illustrations by Ingrid Godon, in muted colours and Dutch-style drawings. It is also a story about the risk of love and loss for anyone, about the possibility of failure, about the joys of hope fulfilled, about fantasy and

escape. And is about the support and love of friends, who continue to wait for us when we have sailed off into the sunset of dreams.
David Nixon, Regional Research Supervisor

King and King and Family

Linda de Haan and Stern Nijand, Berkeley (CA): Tricycle Press

King and King and Family is a twist-and-turn adventure story leading its audience on a journey through the jungle as they follow King and King on their honeymoon adventures. This is a children's storybook that really has it all: a humourous and exciting story placed alongside some fantastic (collage-style) illustrations – each utilising a kaleidoscope of colours to attract and entice readers. Although an 'inclusive' story book based on non-traditional family life, *King and King and Family* is different from the rest – no heavy teaching or preaching here – just a fast-paced story with a very happy ending!
Alexandra Allan, Research Assistant

Prince Cinders

Babette Cole, London: Putnam Juvenile

This book takes the fairytale, *Cinderella*, and turns it on its head by replacing Cinderella with Prince Cinders. Prince Cinders is not a traditional prince, he is '...small, spotty, scruffy and skinny'. Like Cinderella, Prince Cinders spends his days cleaning (including washing his brothers' socks), and dreams of being like his more masculine (and hairy) brothers. When a ('dirty' rather than pristine) fairy tries to help Cinders to achieve his dreams her spell goes wrong, but what we learn is that despite not being conventionally masculine, Prince Cinders will 'get the girl' in the end.

I liked this book because it takes a story everyone is familiar with that is entrenched in British culture and draws on gendered and heterosexualised stereotypes and subverts it in ways which introduces children to the idea that girls and boys and men and women need not act or look like the norm in order to be valued or loved. Using wonderful images and contemporary settings, Prince Cinders challenges the Cinderella myth in a way that also entertains.
Elizabeth Brace, Research Assistant

Spacegirl Pukes
Katy Watson, London: Onlywomen Press Ltd

Spacegirl has two mummies, but that's not what this story is about. The mummies are incidental to the main story, which features a rather original plotline: an outbreak of stomach flu on a rocket ship. The curious juxtaposition of the exotic (space flight) and the cosy (sleeping cats) allows the casual introduction of two mums as perhaps a little of both. The plot does fall somewhat flat at the end, where the ship's own inexplicable ailment is solved by filling up with petrol (yawn) but perhaps children do not expect *dénouement*.

I like the fact that this is not an 'issue' book about the trials and ultimate joys of having lesbian parents but a simple, funny and gleefully disgusting book featuring technicolour yawns and, oh yes, by the way, loving parents who care for you when you are sick.
Renée DePalma, Senior Researcher

William's Doll
Charlotte Zolotow, New York: Harper and Row

William wants a doll to love and nurture as if it were his child. The disclosure activates a range of homophobic responses from family and peers. William is subjected to verbal abuse and provided with stereotypical masculine playthings – a basketball then a train set. William's preference for a feminine toy is acknowledged by his grandmother, who buys the doll and takes issue with William's father. The widening of debates by the grandmother promotes thinking about gendering and the constitution of families. The illustrations identify William as an 'outsider' – his clothes, hair, and poses are clearly different from others. Both text and pictures affirm William's 'right to be'.
Judy Hemingway, Research Assistant

Bystander Anti-discrimination Exercise

Darren Lund

Adapted by Melissa Luhtanen from Arusha Anti-Oppression Workshop

Target group: upper secondary school and university

Subjects: Education, Psychology, Sociology, informal education settings such as respect retreats

Focus: activities to intervene and end oppression, harassment, bullying and discrimination

Duration: approximately two hours

Materials needed: the scenarios given below; ideally some experience with role plays

■ Organise participants into groups of three to six people each

■ Participants will be role-playing a scenario to find a way to intervene and end oppression, harassment, bullying and discrimination

■ Hand out one of the four scenarios to each group. Ask three of the participants to take on a role in the scenario and role-play it as described in the scenario. When the oppression occurs tell the participant that she can choose to react in any constructive way to end the discrimination. This gives participants a chance to think about real life experiences of discrimination and how to intervene in a way that is respectful of the person on the receiving end while still having an impact on the discrimination. It encourages participants to take responsibility for discrimination even if it does not directly affect them

■ Ask the participants to rotate the roles so they get to play them all. During each turn the bystander viewing the discrimination can choose how to react constructively

■ Once all the participants have had a turn, tell the groups that they should choose who will act out the scenario in

160

front of the whole group. Some groups may find a way to incorporate all the participants (in groups of four or more)

- After each group acts out the scenario, the facilitator asks the group questions about their process. As facilitator it is your job to ensure that the solutions have been respectful and haven't created more racism, homophobia, sexism, ableism. If a group comes up with a discriminatory or oppressive solution, the facilitator will have to ask more questions about this solution and steer the group towards greater awareness of the issues affecting that community

- Before starting, emphasise to participants that when they are acting racist, homophobic, ableist, sexist they are not to say pejorative things. Doing so only exacerbates the problems we are trying to address. They can instead say 'Hompohobia, homophobia, homophobia' (or 'racism' or 'ableism' or 'sexism') when enacting the discrimination.

Scenarios

Group One

Roles: white clerk, shopper who is of colour, white bystander

Play: Clerk is rude to shopper who is getting groceries at the till. Bystander watches this and when it is bystander's turn at the till, the clerk all of a sudden becomes friendly. It is obvious that the only reason for the change in attitude is racism. Bystander reacts.

Group Two

Roles: straight spectator; L,G,B, or T pride parader, identity unknown bystander

Play: LGBT pride parader is having a great time marching in the pride parade. Straight spectator starts to heckle from the sidelines. Bystander (who can be in or out of the parade) reacts.

Group Three

Roles: male co-worker, female co-worker, male or female bystander who is a co-worker

Play: Male co-worker sexually harasses female co-worker verbally. Bystander sees this and reacts.

Group Four

Roles: Film festival organiser, potential audience member who uses a wheelchair, board member bystander

Play: A film festival has been organised at a theatre which is not wheelchair accessible. A person who is a potential audience member, and uses a wheelchair, calls the festival for information. The film festival organiser informs the potential audience member that the location is not wheelchair accessible, and therefore the audience member cannot attend. A board member of the film festival overhears the conversation and is appalled that the festival is not accessible to all audiences. The board member bystander reacts.

Using the manual *Different in More Ways Than One* for secondary school students

Stefan Timmermanns

Target group: ages 13 or 14 and above

Subjects: Literature, History, Citizenship – interactive exercises are involved

Focus: awareness of various issues related to the societal reality of being GLBT-identified

Duration: three to six lessons

Material: Various websites (see below) but especially the manual *Different in More Ways than One*

The following proposed programme was conceived for youths aged 13 or 14 and over. Some methods can also be used with younger pupils.

First lesson

To get things started use the method Me / Not Me – Game or, alternatively the Carousel Game (see http://www.diversity-in-europe.org/engl/einleitung/ix_einleitung.htm and click the link Toolbox)

Read a short story

In the manual *Different in More Ways than One* there are short stories in different languages. Read and discuss one of them with your pupils. The following stories reflect the situation of young people who are still in school: chapter 1 Coming out and Identities, chapter 3 Different Lifestyles, chapter 7 The Community (see http://www.diversity-in-europe.org/engl/einleitung/ix_einleitung.htm and click the link Stories).

Imagine...

Aim: To understand why the process of coming out can be very difficult for lesbians, gays and bisexuals.

Method: Pupils divide into small same sex groups. In these groups they have to imagine what would change in their lives if they were gay or lesbian. Give them time to think about this. How would they deal with it? How would their friends react? Are these images positive or negative? Why? Why not?

Please note: This method can be embarrassing for homosexual pupils, especially if they have not yet come out, so care is needed. If someone has difficulty imagining being gay, tell them to imagine that everyone was homosexual and only a few people were straight. What would that be like for those few people?

Alternative suggestion: have the students read an extract of an autobiography by a gay or lesbian author.

Second lesson
The Joneses, the Johnsons and the Johns
Aim: To recognise the concept of family as having different forms.

Method: There are different families with similar sounding names such as Jones, Johnson and John. All have the same number of members (father, mother, son, daughter, etc.). Every pupil receives a card with an identity written on it such as the Johnson father, the Jones daughter, etc; the identities are memorised and the cards handed back. When the group is given the signal to start, the members of the same family have to find each other and then pose for a family photo. Every family shows its pose in front of the others; the pupils outside the group can then try to guess who represents whom in the family.

A second round of the exercise then takes place. This time some cards are changed – unbeknown to the participants. Some families now have different combinations: in one family there are two mothers or two fathers, others are single-parent families, in another the ex-lover of a family member can be integrated. Possible questions for a group discussion include:

■ What was your reaction when you realised that there were two mothers or two fathers in your group?

- Do you know someone who lives with two mothers or fathers?

- What is a family?

- What is important for you in a family?

- What different forms of living together do you know of?

- What is necessary for you to feel at home?

- What kind of living arrangement would you like to have later on in life?

Please note: It is essential that the pupils don't realise that the identities written on the cards have been altered for the second round. To avoid discovery, you might want to use a second set of cards. In the second round, the pupils may initially be irritated if they think the teacher has made a mistake with the identities – 'you put too many mothers in one group!' They may have to be told that this was planned in advance. The exercise is suitable for pupils aged 11 or older.

Hetero, Homo, Bi: pros, cons and stereotypes
Aim: Identifying stereotypes, comparing different forms of partnership

Method: Split the pupils into small groups and distribute a paper divided into the following categories: man-woman relationships, two-man relationships, and two-woman relationships. In small groups pupils are asked to consider the advantages, disadvantages and commonly known stereotypes for each relationship category. The results should be written on the paper and then discussed with the larger group.

Please note: The exercise is appropriate for pupils aged 14 years and over. This exercise works best if they have had relationships of their own or have observed the experiences of others. The teacher can go deeper into the pupils' replies by asking 'Where have you seen examples of this?' The stereotypes should be questioned in a critical way and the restrictions of human perception should be explained.

Third lesson

'From Discrimination to Sexuality'. With this method a discussion on sexual orientation is encouraged without focusing too much on the topic of sexuality. In addition, this method offers the opportunity to talk about commonalities and differences among different grounds for discrimination (for a description see: http://www.diversity-in-europe.org/engl/einleitung/ix_einleitung.htm and click the link 'Toolbox').

Alternatively, or if you want to discuss religious feelings towards homosexuality, you could use the method 'Write to Christina' (see the same link as above). Youths write an answer to the letter of a young Catholic lesbian asking for advice. For those who choose this method, it is highly recommended that they become informed about the attitude of the different churches towards homosexuality, for example by reading chapter 9 of the manual *Different in More Ways Than One*.

This text contains excerpts from the handbook *Different in More Ways Than One: Providing Guidance for Teenagers on Their Way to Identity, Sexuality and Respect*, which was published in 2004 by the former Ministry for Health, Social Affairs, Women and Family in the state of North Rhine-Westphalia. The book was created with support from the European Union in collaboration with partners in France, Italy, the Netherlands and Austria. The handbook was not part of North Rhine-Westphalian government's public relations activities.

Hiding your sexual orientation

Michele Kahn

Target group: Upper secondary school and university

Subjects: Education, Psychology, Sociology

Focus: The activity is designed to impress upon students how diffi-cult and exhausting it is to hide sexual orientation

Duration: One to one and a half hours

Materials needed: Tokens (pennies, marbles, chips, etc) bell

Procedure:

1. Organise students into groups of 3 or 4 and ask them to discuss the following questions, which can be adjusted to meet the needs of the course. The purpose is to gauge students' opinions about the role sexual orientation plays in daily life as well as to establish the topic.

    ■ Should students know about their teacher's sexual orienta-tion? Why or why not?

    ■ Is sexual orientation relevant in the workplace? Why or why not?

After the small group discussions, ask a representative from each group to summarise some of the opinions that were shared.

2. Distribute three to five tokens to each student depending on the class size and provide the following written instructions.

> For the next 20 minutes you will discuss one of the topics below or an alternative topic.
>
> Under no circumstances say anything that would reveal your sexual orientation. If you do you must relinquish a token to the person you are speaking to.

167

At the sound of the bell find another person to continue the discussion with.

Possible topics:

- Do proms reinforce traditional gender norms? Should they be eliminated? Why or why not?

- Should lesbian, gay, and bisexual people be allowed to marry or have the same rights as married people but under a different name?

- In many countries the age of consent for girls and boys differs. In your opinion, what should the consent age be and should it differ depending on gender?

- How should a person decide who to marry?

- Does true love exist?

Every three to five minutes the students should change conversation partners. A bell signals to students that it's time to change. Adjust or change the conversation topics as needed but for the purpose of this activity all should be related to gender or sexual orientation. If desired, instructors can provide incentives in the form of 'prizes' or points. If this is the case, instructors will notice that some students will actively try to get the tokens by asking questions in such a way as to make the other person reveal their sexual orientation.

3. Post-activity discussion questions: students return to their discussion groups and share answers to the following questions:

- How difficult was it not to reveal your sexual orientation?

- Did hiding your sexual orientation detract from or influence what you were saying? If so, how?

- Who had the fewest tokens? What made it so difficult to keep the tokens?

- Who had the most tokens? What strategies did they use to collect them?

Following the small group discussions get a representative from each group to summarise some of the experiences that were shared.

Homophobia in our community: must coming out mean losing family?

Melinda L. de Jesús

Target group: University and upper secondary school

Subjects: Asian-Pacific American studies, Queer Studies, American Studies, Sociology, Psychology, History, Anthropology, Comparative Literature, Multicultural education

Focus: Identity, family and culture and the relationship to GLBT issues

Duration: Several lessons

Material:

- Chapter: Karin Aguilar-San Juan's *Going Home: Enacting Justice in Queer Asian America* in David Eng and Alice Hom's (eds) *Q&A: Queer in Asian America* (Temple University Press, 1998)

- Screen: *Love Ltd* a short independent film by Jennifer Thuy Lan Phang (1999) Available: http://cart.frameline.org/ ProductDetails.asp?ProductCode=T523 Synopsis: A sister and brother turn a dysfunctional family dinner into an unappreciated coming out party. Love Ltd confronts homophobia through a quirky, unrelenting tale about the things we choose to say – or not say – to the people we love.

Background

Like my chapter, this lesson plan focuses on homophobia in Asian-Pacific American communities but much of what is said here applies to other communities as well. In fact, the distance created by the book and the film might even allow students from other communities to engage more easily in discussion.

Many Asian Pacific Americans view their families as havens from the racism of mainstream American society. However, queer Asian Pacific Americans fear losing this haven should they decide to come out to their families. Jennifer Phang's short film, *Love Ltd*, a farcical suburban dramedy, takes a close look at the repercussions of coming out for two Asian Pacific American siblings and asks if the desire to belong to one's family comes at too high a price.

Discussion questions about the film and chapter

This film includes scenes with gay and lesbian content. If the teacher or instructor is straight, I realise some people may feel uncomfortable. Straight people using the film need to consider that this is just 27 minutes of discomfort versus a lifetime of discomfort for Asian Pacific Americans and those from many other communities who can't come out to their own families.

- Given that the United States and other western societies are heterosexually-biased, privileging heterosexuality in all forms of cultural production, how does this film inform us of the issues facing gays and lesbians in the Asian Pacific American community and can we then translate these experiences to other communities?

- Do you consider your family a safe haven? Describe the role of the family in this film. What does it take to belong?

- By the film's end, who gets to stay and who has to leave? Why? What do you think the film-maker is trying to get across to the audience?

- How does this film illuminate the complicated intersection of identity, family and culture? Can you relate the struggles shown here to those of other parallel cultures or communities? How are they similar or different?

References

AHBAB (GLAS news archive 1996-1997)

Ali, S (2003) To Be a Girl: culture and class in schools. *Gender and Education* 15(3) p269-83

Alberta Human Rights and Citizenship Commission. (2000) *Tools for Transformation: Human Rights Education and Diversity Initiatives in Alberta*. Edmonton, AB: Government of Alberta

Alberta Teachers' Association. (2006) Diversity, equity and human rights [on-line]. Accessed 9 February, 2006

Alternet (2003) Out of the Koran (By Rachel Giese). Accessed 22 June. http://www.teachers.ab.ca/Issues+In+Education/Diversity+and+Human+Rights/

Anderson, S (2000) Stockwell Day ruined my life. *Now Magazine* [Electronic version]. 16 November, Accessed 9 February, 2006, from http://www.nowtoronto.com/issues/2000-11-16/newsspread.html

Apple, M (2006) Critical theory today: Visions from the visionaries. Paper presented at the annual meeting of the American Educational Research Association, 7-11 April, San Francisco

Ashley, J (2001) History of Racism at the University of Vermont. <http://www.uvm.edu/~jashley/history5.html> Accessed 7 December 2002

Asia Source (2001) Special Report: Asian Americans and the Census 2000 Results. 30 May 2001. <http://www.asiasource.org/news/at_mp_02.cfm?newsid=53011> Accessed 30 January 2007.

Back, G (1985) *Are you still my mother: Are you still my family?* New York: Warner Books, Inc

Blair, M (2001) *Why Pick on Me? school exclusion and Black youth.* Stoke-on-Trent: Trentham Books

Bloom, BS (1984) *Taxonomy of educational objectives.* Boston, MA: Allyn and Bacon

Boshenek, M and Brown, W (2001) *Hatred in the hallways: Violence and discrimination against lesbian, gay, bisexual and transgender students in U.S. schools.* New York, NY: Human Rights Watch. Accessed 10 April, 2006 from: http://www.hrw.org/reports/2001/uslgbt/

Buijs, FJ and Rath, J (2002) Muslims in Europe: The State of Research. Essay for the Russell Sage Foundation: New York

Butler, J (1990) *Gender Trouble. Feminism and the subversion of identity.* Tenth anniversary edition. London: Routledge

Canadian Race Relations Foundation. (2001) *CRRF 2001 Best Practices Reader* Toronto, ON: Author

Carrington, B and Short, G (1989) *Race and the Primary School: Theory into Practice.* Windsor: National Foundation for Educational Research

Caster, P (1998) Rights law now protects gays: Decision is fair, says activist. *Red Deer Advocate*, 9 April, A1-2

Caudillo v. Lubbock Independent School District, 5:03-CV-165-C (Northern Dist. Texas, 3 March, 2004)

Chasnoff, D (1996) It's elementary: talking about gay issues in school [video-recording]. In HS Cohen and D. Chasnoff (Producer): New Day Films

CBS News (2004a) *Book battles: Evolution, marriage.* 8 November, Accessed 30 December, 2005 from (http://www.cbsnews.com/stories/2004/10/27/tech/main 651777.shtml)

CBS News (2005) *Texas may ban gay foster parents.* 20 April, Accessed 30 December, 2005 from (http://www.cbsnews.com/stories/2005/04/20/national/ main689771.shtml)

Centro de Investigaciones Sociológicas (CIS) (2004) *Barómetro de junio.* Estudio nº 2.568. Madrid: CIS.

Coard, B (1971) *How the West Indian child is made educationally subnormal in the British school system: the scandal of the black child in schools in Britain,* London, New Beacon for the Caribbean Education and Community Workers' Association

COGAM (1996/97) *Investigación sobre las actitudes hacia la homosexualidad en la población adolescente escolarizada de la Comunidad de Madrid*

COGAM (1999) *Familias de Hecho: situación social de las familias formadas por lesbianas, gays, y sus hijos*

COGAM (1999) *25 cuestiones sobre la orientación sexual*

COGAM (2005) *Homofobia en el Sistema educativo*

COGAM (2006) *Guías con CCOO: Diferentes Formas de Amar* (para profesores), El amor y el sexo no son de un solo color (para adolescentes)

COGAM documents can be consulted at: www.cogam.org/educacion/ documentos (2 Oct, 2006) *Le Monde de William* can be found at: <http://www. exaequo.be/media/d_EXAbrochwillam_89590.pdf> (Accessed 2 Oct, 2006).

Cotton, K (2001) Developing empathy in children and youth. *School Improvement Research Series*, Northwest Regional Educational Laboratory, Portland, Oregon

Crawford, E (1993) *Over my track.* Victoria: Penguin

Crozier, G (2003) Researching Black parents: Making sense of the role of research and the researcher. *Qualitative Research* 3(1) p79-94

Dadzie, S (2000) *Toolkit for Tackling Racism in Schools.* Stoke-on-Trent: Trentham

Dawidowicz, LS (1975) *The war against the Jews, 1933-1945* (1st ed.). New York: Holt Rinehart and Winston

Deacon, R, Morrell, R and Prinsloo, J (1999) Discipline and Homophobia in South African Schools: The Limits of Legislated Transformation. In *A Dangerous Knowing: Sexuality, Pedagogy and Popular Culture* D. Epstein and J. T. Sears (eds) London: Cassell

de Jesús, ML (2005) A walkin'' fo de (Rice) Kake: A Filipina American Feminist's Adventures in Academia or, A Pinay's Progress.' In *Pinay Power: Feminist Critical Theory: Theorizing the Filipina/American Experience.* ML de Jesús (ed) New York: Routledge, p259-274

de Jesús, ML (2002) Rereading History, Rewriting Desire: Tracing Queerness in Carlos Bulosan's *America Is in the Heart* and Bienvenido Santos' *Scent of Apples. The Journal of Asian American Studies* 5(2) p91-111

de Jesús, ML (1999) Transforming Pedagogy: Integrating New Media Technologies and Asian American Studies. *Works and Days: Special Issue on Teaching and Technology,* 16 (1-2) p291-308

DePalma, R and Atkinson, E (2006a) *Permission to talk about it: LGB and straight teachers' narratives of sexualities equality.* Paper presented at the annual meeting of the British Educational Research Association, 6-9 September, University of Warwick

DePalma, R and Atkinson, E (2006b). The sound of silence: Talking about sexual orientation and schooling. *Sex Education* 6(4) p333-349

Department for Education and Skills and Department of Health. (2004). Stand up for Us. Accessed 30 September, 2006 from www.wiredforhealth.gov.uk/standup forus

Different in More Ways Than One (2004) Providing guidance for Teenagers on Their Way to Identity, Sexuality and Respect; Editor: Ministry for Health, Social Affairs, Women and Family of the federal state of North Rhine Westphalia. Düsseldorf. Internet: www.diversity-in-europe.org .

Dishonoring Texas. (13 June) *Washington Post,* A18

Dijk, L van (1995) *Damned Strong Love – the true story of Stephan K. and Willi, G.* New York: Henry Holt

Donner, C (1992 and 2006) *Les letters de mon petit frere.* Paris: Ecole des loisirs

Douglas, N, Warwick, I, Kemp, S and Whitty, G (1997) *Playing it Safe: Responses of Secondary School Teachers to Lesbian, Gay and Bisexual Pupils, Bullying, HIV and AIDS Education and Section 28.* London: Institute of Education, University of London

Echoing Green (2006) http://www.echoinggreen.org/index.cfm?fuseaction=Page. viewPageandpageId=666. Accessed 15 February, 2007

Eisenberg, N and Fabes, RA (1998) Prosocial development. In W. Damon (series ed) and N. Eisenberg (Vol. ed), *Handbook of child psychology: Vol. 3. Social, emotional, and personality development* (fifth ed, pp 701-778). New York: Wiley

Ellis, V, and High, S (2004) Something more to tell you: gay, lesbian or bisexual young people's experiences of secondary schooling. *British Educational Research Journal* 30(2) p214 – 225

Epstein, D (1998) "Real boys don't work': boys' 'underachievement', masculinities and the harassment of sissies.' Pp 96-108 in *Failing Boys? Issues in Gender and Achievement*. D. Epstein, J. Elwood, V. Hey and JM Buckingham (eds) Open University Press

Epstein, D, O'Flynn, S and Telford, D. (2003) *Silenced Sexualities in Schools and Universities*. Stoke-on-Trent: Trentham Books

Epstein, D, Hewitt, R, Leonard, D, Mauthner, M and Watkins, C (2003) Avoiding the Issue: Homophobia, School Policies and Identities in Secondary Schools. In C. Vincent (ed) *Identity, Social Justice and Education*. London: RoutledgeFalmer

Epstein, D and Johnson, R (1998) *Schooling Sexualities*. Buckingham: Open University Press

Epstein, D and Sealey, A (1990) *'Where it Really Matters ... Developing Anti-Racist Education in Predominantly White Primary Schools*. Birmingham: Development Education Centre

First Amendment Center (2006) Public Schools and Sexual Orientation: A First Amendment framework for finding common ground. First Amendment Center consensus guidelinesAccessed 29 September, 2006, from http://www.first amendmentcenter.org/about.aspx?id=16611

Foucault, M (1988) *Madness and civilization: A history of insanity in the age of reason*. New York: Vintage

Frank, B (1987) Hegemonic heterosexual masculinity. *Studies in Political Economy* 24 p159-70

Frank, B (1993 Straight/strait Jackets for Masculinity: Educating for Real Men. *Atlantis* 18 p47-59

Friend, RA (1993) Choices, Not Closets: Heterosexism and Homophobia in Schools. In *Beyond Silenced Voices: Class, Race, and Gender in United States Schools,* L Weis and M Fine (eds) New York: State University of New York Press

Gaine, C (1987) *No Problem Here: A Practical Approach to Education and Race in White Schools*. London: Hutchinson

Gaine, C (1996) *Still No Problem Here*. Stoke-on-Trent: Trentham Books

Gaine, C (2005) *We're All White, Thanks: the persisting myth about white schools*. Stoke-on-Trent: Trentham Books

GALOP (1998) *Telling it Like it Is ... Lesbian, Gay and Bisexual Youth Speak Out on Homphobic Violence.* London: GALOP

Ganguly, M (2002) *Ganz normal anders – lesbisch, schwul, bi: Lebenskunde Sonderheft zur Integration gleichgeschlechtlicher Lebensweisen,* Berlin: Humanistischer Verband Deutschlands. Available from: iku@humanis mus.de

Gilbert, R and Gilbert, P (1998) *Masculinity Goes to School.* Sydney: Allen and Unwin.

Gillborn, D (1990) *'Race', ethnicity and education: teaching and learning in multi-ethnic schools.* London: Unwin Hyman

Gleitzmann, M (2006) *Two Weeks with the Queen.* Puffin Books and Pearson Education

Grace, AP and Wells, K (2001) Getting an education in Edmonton, Alberta: The case of queer youth. *Torquere: Journal of the Canadian Lesbian and Gay Studies Association* 3 p34-44

Hall, S (1996) Introduction: Who Needs 'Identity'? in *Questions of Cultural Identity,* In S. Hall and P du Gay (eds) London: Sage

Harvey, L (1990) *Critical Social Research.* London: Unwin Hyman

Haynes, SR (2002) *Noah's curse: the biblical justification of American slavery.* Oxford; New York: Oxford University Press

Health sevices/ technology assessment text (n.d.) Accessed December 31, 2005, from http://www.ncbi.nlm.nih.gov/books/bv.fcgi?rid=hstat5.table.67642

Helie, A (2007) Muslim religious and GLBT strategies. ILGA files http://www.ilga.org/news_results.asp?LanguageID=1andFileCategory=1andFileID=877 Accessed 30 March, 2007

Hey, V (1997) *The Company She Keeps: An Ethnography of Girls' Friendships.* Buckingham: Open University Press

Holy hatred? Penalties for homosexuality in Muslim Countries. http://www.lolapress.org/elec2/artenglish/heli_e.htm. Accessed 4 February, 2007

hooks, B (1994) *Teaching to Transgress: Education as the Practice of Freedom.* New York: Routledge

Huriyah (2006) Interview with Muhsin Hendricks. Accessed 5 January, 2007

Jennett, M, with contributions by Rivers, I, Jowett, Kirsten, Power, P and Caught, R (2004) *Stand Up for Us: Challenging Homophobia in Schools.* London: National Health Schools Standard (Crown Copyright)

Joireman, J (2004) Empathy and the self-absorption paradox II: Self-rumination and self-reflection as mediators between shame, guilt, and empathy. *Self and Identity* 3(3) p225-238

Kennedy, C (2000) New student group fights anti-gay bias at local high school. *Red Deer Advocate,* 20 November, A1

Kinsella, W (2001) *Web of hate: Inside Canada's far right network* (2nd. ed.). Toronto, ON: Harper Collins

Knapp, S (2006) Prof battles injustice despite threats. *OnCampus*, 3(16) Accessed 10 April, 2006 from http://www.ucalgary.ca/oncampus/weekly/march3-06/lund. html

Knowles, E and Ridley, W (2006) *Another Spanner in the Works: challenging prejudice and racism in mainly white schools.* Stoke-on-Trent: Trentham Books

Kossowan, B (1994) Sex with children 'next step': Pedophiles may seek rights-Day. *Red Deer Advocate*, 15 April, A1-2

Kreuzpaintner, M (2004) *Sommersturm,* film, 98 minutes, Germany. X Verleih

Legg, J (2006) Toddlers now using homophobic abuse, says union. *Times Educational Supplement*, 21 July

Letts IV, WJ and Sears, JT (1999) Queering Elementary Education: Advancing the Dialogue about Sexualities and Schooling. Lanham, MD: Rowman and Littlefield

Levy, SR, Freitas, AL and Salovey, P (2002) Construing action abstractly and blurring social distinctions: Implications for perceiving homogeneity among, but also empathizing with and helping, others. *Journal of Personality and Social Psychology* 83 p1224-1238

Louie, S and Omatsu, G (eds) (2001) *Asian Americans: The Movement and the Moment.* Los Angeles: UCLA Asian American Studies Center Press

Lund, DE (1998) Social justice activism in a conservative climate: Students and teachers challenging discrimination in Alberta. *Our Schools/Our Selves* 9(4) p24-38

Lund, DE (2002) Fostering dignity and respect in Red Deer. *Just in Time: News from the Diversity, Equity and Human Rights Committee* 1(2) p3

Lund, DE (2003) Facing the challenges: Student antiracist activists counter backlash and stereotyping. *Teaching Education Journal* 14 p265-278

Lund, DE (2005) Promoting dignity and respect in Red Deer: Forming Alberta's first Gay/Straight Alliance. In N. O'Haire (ed) *Lessons learned: A collection of stories and articles about bisexual, gay, lesbian, transgender issues* (p57-62). Ottawa, ON: Canadian Teachers' Federation

Lyotard, JF (1979) *The postmodern condition: A report on knowledge.* Minneapolis: University of Minnesota Press

Mac an Ghaill, M (1994a) (In)visibility: Sexuality, Race and Maculinity in the School Context. In *Challenging Lesbian and Gay Inequalities in Education*, D. Epstein (ed) Buckingham: Open University Press

Mac an Ghaill, M (1994b) *The Making of Men: Masculinities, Sexualities and Schooling.* Buckingham: Open University Press

Mac an Ghaill, M (2000) Rethinking (Male) Gendered Sexualities in Education: What About the British Heteros? *The Journal of Men's Studies* 8 p195-212

MacGillivray, IK (2004) Gay rights and school policy: A case study in community factors that facilitate or impede educational change. *International Journal of Qualitative Studies in Education* 17(3) p347-370

McIntosh, P (1988) White privilege and male privilege: A personal account of coming to see correspondences through work in women's studies. In M Andersen and PH Collins (eds) *Race, Class, and Gender: An anthology*. Belmont, CA, Wadsworth Publishing

Macpherson, W (1999) *The Stephen Lawrence inquiry: report of an inquiry by Sir William Macpherson of Cluny* London: HMSO

Martino, W (1999) 'Cool boys,' 'party animals,' 'squids,' and 'poofters': Interrogating the Dynamics and Politics of Adolescent Masculinities in School. *British Journal of Sociology of Education* 20 p239-63

Martino, W (2000) Policing Masculinities: Investigating the Role of Homophobia and Heteronormativity in the Lives of Adolescent School Boys. *The Journal of Men's Studies* 8 p213-36

Marx, K (1963) *The 18th Brumaire of Louis Bonaparte.* New York: International Publishers

Mikkelson, B and Mikkelson, D (2004) Urban legends reference pages. Accessed 30 December, 2005, from http://www.snopes.com/politics/religion/drlaura.asp

Metro Weekly (2006) A man for all seasons

Mirza, HS (2006) 'Race', Gender and Educational Desire. *Race, Ethnicity and Education* 9(2) p137-58

Nakashima, SK (2002) Rantage-APA Style.'10 October 2002. <http://ryochan.diaryland.com/021010_2.html> 5 December 2002.

Nawas, A (1979) *Le Vin, le Vent, la Vie* (translated from Arabic by Vincent Mansour Monteil, Paris: Sindbad

Nayak, A and Kehily, M (1997) Masculinities and Schooling: Why are Young Men so Homophobic? In *Border Patrols: Policing the Boundaries of Heterosexuality*. D. L. Steinberg, D. Epstein and R. Johnson (eds) London: Cassell http://www.metroweekly.com/feature/?ak=2458. Accessed 15 February, 2007.

NSPCC. (2006) Calls to ChildLine about sexual orientation, homophobia and homophobic bullying.Accessed 27 September, 2006, from http://www.nspcc.org.uk/inform/publications/downloads/WD_CasenotesSexualOrientation_gf37413.pdf #search=%22NSPCC%20homophobic%20Bullying%20Childline%22

Ofsted (2002) *Sex and Relationships: A report from the Office of Her Majesty's Chief Inspector of Schools*. p43. London: Ofsted

Okin, SM, Cohen, J, Howard, M and Nussbaum, MC (1999) *Is multiculturalism bad for women?* Princeton, N.J.: Princeton University Press

Osajima, K (1998) Pedagogical Considerations in Asian American Studies. *The Journal of Asian American Studies* 1(3) p269-292

Quinlivan, K and Town, S (1999) Queer as Fuck?: Exploring the potential of queer pedagogies in researching school experiences of lesbian and gay youth. In *A Dangerous Knowing: Sexuality, Pedagogy and Popular Culture*. D. Epstein and J. T. Sears (eds) London: Cassell

Peirce, CS (1877) The fixation of belief. In P. P. Wiener (ed) *Charles S. Peirce: Selected writings*. New York: Dover Publications

Pruegger, V and Kiely, J (2002) *Perceptions of racism and hate activities among youth in Calgary: Effects on the lived experience*. Calgary, AB: City of Calgary

Purves, L (2006) Homophobic bullying. The Learning Curve, 2 October, BBC Radio 4

Renold, E (2005) *Girls, boys, and junior sexualities: exploring children's gender and sexual relations in the primary school*. London; New York: RoutledgeFalmer

Riddle, D (1985) Homophobia scale. In *Opening doors to understanding and acceptance*. K. Obear and A. Reynolds (eds). Boston: Unpublished essay

Rivers, I (1995) The Victimisation of Gay Teenagers in Schools: Homophobia in Education. *Pastoral Care* p35-41

Roca, J (2003) Ni niños sin sexo, ni sexo sin niños: el modelo sexual hegemónico católico en versión española. In Guasch, O and Viñuales, O (ed) *Sexualidades. Diversidad y control social*. Barcelona: Bellaterra

Rogers, C (1980) *A Way of Being*. Boston: Houghton Mifflin

Rudolph, JL (2005) Epistemology for the masses: the origins of 'The Scientific Method' in American schools. *History of Education Quarterly* 45(3) p341-376

Safe Schools Coalition (2004) GLBT Civil and Human Rights in Brief in Schools and Families. Accessed 30 December, 2005 from http://www.safeschoolscoalition. org/lawpolicy-fed-case-constitution.html#1)

Sanjakar, F (2005) Developing an Appropriate Sexual Health Education Curriculum Framework for Muslim Students. In B. van Driel (ed) *Confronting Islamophobia in Educational Practice*, pp 143-161

(SCP) Sociaal Cultureel Planbureau (2006) *Gewoon Doen*. The Hague

Sears, JT (1999) Teaching queerly: Some elementary propositions. In W. J. Letts and J. T. Sears (eds) *Queering elementary education: advancing the dialogue about sexualities and schooling* (pp 3-14). Lanham, Md.: Rowman and Littlefield

Sherwin, A (2006) Gay means rubbish, says BBC. 6 June, The Times Online

Skeggs, B (1997) *Formations of Class and Gender*. London: Sage

Somekh, B (2005) *Transforming professional knowledge through a global action research community*. Paper presented at the First Congress for Qualitative Inquiry, 5-7 May, University of Illinois

Spain LOGSE (1990) *Ley Orgánica 1/1990 de Ordenación General del Sistema educativo, de 3 de octubre Boletín Oficial del Estad*, (4/10/ 1990) http://www. orozco.cc/Educa/Docus/sis_educ/texto_vigenteLOgseE.htm (Accessed 2 Oct, 2006)

Spain LOE (2006) Ley Orgánica 2/2006 de Educación, de 3 de mayo' *Boletín Oficial del Estado* n. 106 (4/5/2006)<http://www.boe.es/g/es/bases_datos/ doc.php?coleccion=iberlexandid=2006/07899 (Accessed 2 Oct, 2006)

REFERENCES

Sturmer, S, Synder, M and Omoto, AM (2005) Prosocial emotions and helping: The moderating role of group membership. *Journal of Personality and Social Psychology* 88 p532-546

Texas Education Agency (2003) *Minutes, State Board of Education*. 7 November, Accessed 30 December, 2005 from http://www.tea.state.tx.us/sboe/ minutes/sboe/2003/1107min.doc)

The Pew Research Center (2006) Pew Poll released 22 March, 2006

Thorne, B (1993) *Gender play: Girls and boys in school*. New Brunswick, NJ: Rutgers University Press

Timmermanns, S (2003) *Keine Angst, die beissen nicht! Evaluation schwul-lesbischer Aufklärungsprojekte in Schulen*, Norderstedt: Books on Demand

Tompkins, P (1981) *Symbols of heresy in the magic of obelisks*. New York: Harper

Troyna, B and Hatcher, R (1992) *Racism in Children's Lives: A Study of Mainly-White Primary Schools*. London, Routledge

Vries, J de (1998) *Verschillen Verkend*. Utrecht: Forum

Whitaker, B (1996) *Unspeakable Love: Gay and Lesbian Life in the Middle East*. Saqi Books

Williams, T, Connolly, J, Pepler, D and Craig, W (2005) Peer victimization, social support, and psychosocial adjustment of sexual minority adolescents. *Journal of Youth and Adolescence* 34 (5) p471-482

Willis, P (1977) *Learning to Labour: How Working Class Kids Get Working Class Jobs*. Alsdershot: Saxon House

YWCA England and Wales. *Pride not Prejudice*. Accessed 2 October, 2006, from http://www.ywca-gb.org.uk/briefings.asp

Zielinsky, S (2002) Gay teenager beaten: Victim fearful attackers could return. *Red Deer Advocate*, 4 July, A1

Educational support websites

Affirmation Gay and Lesbian Mormons http://www.affirmation.org/

Affirmation: United Methodists for Lesbian, Gay, and Transgender Concerns http://umaffirm.org/

Al-bab: http://www.al-bab.com/

Alberta Teachers Association http://www.teachers.ab.ca/Issues+In+Education/Diversity+and+Human+Rights/Sexual+Orientation/Index.htm

Al Fatiha (http://www.al-fatiha.org

Aswat http://www.aswatgroup.org/english/

Behind the Mask: http://www.mask.org.za

Bint el Nas http://www.bintelnas.org/

Colombia Diversa: http://www.proyectocolombiadiversa.org/

COGAM http://www.cogam.org/

Department of Education and Skills http://www.dfes.gov.uk/search/results/kbsearch?qt=homophobia&sc=dfes&ha=1

Different in More Ways Than One. Providing Guidance for Teenagers on Their Way to Identity, Sexuality and Respect www.diversity-in-europe.org

Dignidade: http://www.grupodignidade.org.br/

The Evangelical Fellowship for Lesbian and Gay Christians (EFLGC) http://www.eflgc.org.uk/who.shtml

GASA (and GALA) http://www.wits.ac.za/gala/archives_g.htm

Gay and Lesbian Arabic Society (GLAS) www.glas.org

GLSEN: www.glsen.org

Helem www.helem.net

Huriyah http://www.huriyahmag.com

Imaan http://www.imaan.org.uk/

The Jewish Gay and Lesbian Group (JGLG) http://www.jglg.org.uk/

KAOS GL www.kaosgl.com

Lambda Istanbul http://www.qrd.org/qrd/www/world/europe/turkey/

LesMigraS http://www.lesmigras.de/index.html

Merhaba: http://www.merhaba.be

Metropolitan Community Churches http://www.mccchurch.org

Middle East Blogspot http://gaymiddleeast.blogspot.com

The Miles Project: http://www.berlin.lsvd.de/cms/index.php?option=com_content&task=view&id=22&Itemid=64)

NAZ Foundation: http://www.nfi.net/

No Outsiders http://www.nooutsiders.sunderland.ac.uk/

Pride and Prejudice Program http://www.prideandprejudice.com.au/

Organisation Q (http://www.queer.ba/udruzenjeq/en/udruzenje.htm)

Queer Jihad www.queerjihad.com

Quest http://www.questgaycatholic.org.uk/home.asp

Safra Project: http://www.safraproject.org

SchLAue Kiste (Clever Box) http://www.google.be/search?hl=en&q=Schlaue+Kiste&btnG=Google+Search&meta=

Schools Out http://www.schools-out.org.uk/

Stand up for us http://www.wiredforhealth.gov.uk/PDF/stand_up_for_us_04.pdf

TANDIS (Tolerance and Non-Discrimination Information System) (http://tandis.odihr.pl/?p=ki-ho)

Triangle Project http://www.triangle.org.za/

Yoesuf: http://www.yoesuf.nl

Index